The Black Infantry
in the West
1869-1891

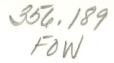

The Black Infantry in the West 1869-1891

ARLEN L. FOWLER

Foreword by William H. Leckie

With a new Foreword to the 1996 Edition

University of Oklahoma Press
Norman and London

Library of Congress Cataloging-in-Publication Data

Fowler, Arlen L.
    The Black infantry in the West : 1869–1891 / Arlen L. Fowler :
foreword by William H. Leckie. — With a new foreword to the 1996
ed.
        p. cm.
    Originally published: Westport, Conn. : Greenwood Pub. Corp.,
1971.
    Includes bibliographical references and index.
    ISBN 0-8061-2883-6 (alk. paper)
        1. Afro–American soldiers—West (U.S.)—History—19th century.
2. United States. Army—Afro-American troops—History—19th
century. 3. United States. Army. Infantry—History—19th century.
4. West (U.S.)—History—1860–1890. I. Title.
E185.63.F66 1996
356'.189'08996073—dc20   96-14945
                                                                    CIP

The Black Infantry in the West, 1869–1891, by Arlen L. Fowler,
was originally published in hardcover by Greenwood Publishing Group, Inc., Westport, CT, 1971. Copyright © 1971 by
Arlen L. Fowler. This edition by arrangement with Greenwood Publishing Group, Inc. All rights reserved.

Oklahoma Paperbacks edition published 1996 by the University of Oklahoma Press, Norman, Publishing Division of the
University. Foreword to the 1996 Edition by William H. Leckie
copyright © 1996 by the University of Oklahoma Press. All
rights reserved. Manufactured in the U.S.A. First printing of
the University of Oklahoma Press edition, 1996.

1   2   3   4   5   6   7   8   9   10

*To my mother and father
and my wife and children*

Contents

Illustrations

Foreword

The military contributions of black Americans in the wars of our country have, until recently, received scant attention. Now, with rising interest in every facet of the black experience, books and articles approach floodtide, and most Americans are becoming aware that black men have bled and died in every war this nation has fought. The deeds of these men from the American Revolution to the current struggle in Vietnam are being researched, recorded, and integrated into the mainstream of our country's history. Their role in the conquest of the trans-Mississippi West during the last half of the nineteenth century is no exception.

Nearly 200,000 black soldiers fought in the Civil War to gain freedom for their people, and, as the records amply show, they fought well. After that bloody struggle, Congress enacted legislation providing for an experiment using Negro soldiers as part of the regular army. Six regiments, two of cavalry and four of infantry were authorized. Designated as the Ninth and Tenth cavalries and the Thirty-eighth, Thirty-ninth, Fortieth, and Forty-first infantries, these units were organized and armed under white officers between the summers of 1866 and 1867.

The cavalry moved west to the Texas and Kansas frontiers in the spring and summer of 1867. For the next generation they campaigned and buried their dead the length and breadth of the Great Plains, in Arizona and Colorado. Called "buffalo soldiers" by their Indian antagonists, they earned a place in our military annals sufficient to gain them, today, long delayed recognition and to be regularly portrayed on the television screen. No such plaudits have been accorded the infantry, though they followed hard on the heels of the cavalry. By 1869 army reorganization had merged the four regiments into two—the Twenty-fourth and the Twenty-fifth—and both were assigned to the turbulent Texas frontier. Two long decades later they were still in the West but had garnered little mention. Their duties were essential but more often dull than exciting. Escorting trains and stages, building roads and telegraph lines, guarding waterholes and protecting lines of supply are not activities that excite the newspaper reporter. Only on rare occasions did a firefight enliven the monotony of their lives. For this reason, though they made footprints from the muddy Rio Grande to the Canadian border, their story has received little attention and our history is the poorer for it. In the pages that follow, historian Arlen Fowler has gone far toward filling this gap by giving us, for the first time, a scholarly history of the Negro infantry in the West.

Much of Professor Fowler's story is of necessity taken from official records, for there is little other material. This is not surprising when one realizes that the men of whom he writes were mostly illiterate and therefore left little in the way of letters, diaries, journals, or memoirs. The remaining sources are scattered newspaper items, brief regimental histories, and passing references in a few books. The day-to-day lives of the men and their families, their hopes and aspirations, their sorrows and joys, form all but blank pages that defy the researcher. Even photographs are rare, for apparently frontier photographers had little interest in black soldiers. Nevertheless, Professor Fowler has written an integrated narrative of the officers and men of the Twenty-fourth and Twenty-fifth infantries between the years 1869 and 1891 that will be of lasting value.

All troops stationed in far west Texas or along the meandering Rio Grande faced common enemies: marauding Indians sweeping southward from reservations in Indian Territory, rancheros attacking from New Mexico or from nests in Mexico, Mexican outlaws and revolutionaries, white gunmen, cattle rustlers, and horse thieves. Against these, in time, the blue-clad soldiers were successful. In addition, the black soldier faced the obstacles of prejudice and discrimination, both within and without the army. These twin foes plagued his every step and proved to be the only obstacles he could not surmount. The black response could have been a swift loss of pride, a breakdown of morale, or mass desertion, followed by quick action by the army high command to end the experiment. However, as Fowler points out, none of these occurred. On the contrary, forged in the elements of a lawless frontier, the black regiments emerged as tough, disciplined, and effective units. The desertion rates were among the lowest in the army and alcoholism, the curse of the frontier, was rare among black regulars. Regimental pride and morale were high.

Comparative peace came to the Texas frontier in 1880 and the Twenty-fourth was transferred to Indian Territory with the Twenty-fifth moving north to the Department of Dakota. Now there was time for grizzled veterans to regale recruits with stories of their grim sweep of the Staked Plains with Shafter in 1875, of a stealthy march across the Rio Grande into Mexico after Kickapoos or of the grinding pursuit of the great Apache chief Victorio. The Twenty-fifth remained in the north until the close of the period while the Twenty-fourth marched west to Arizona in 1888 and remained until the curtain closed on that frontier.

In the course of his narrative Fowler draws attention to the efforts of devoted chaplains, notably Allen Allensworth and George Mullins, to educate their charges. In so doing they did much to provide an understanding and a framework for educational programs through the army.

By any standard, the experiment begun in 1866 with Negro regulars proved a success. It is unfortunate that the contributions of these soldiers and the lessons learned were so little known and appreciated by the American people of their time. A century has passed since these black men in blue campaigned to bring peace and order in the West, and a book such as Professor Fowler's is long overdue. Now, at last, light has driven one more shadow from the pages of American history.

WILLIAM H. LECKIE

March 1970

Foreword to the 1996 Edition

Arlen Fowler's book on the Twenty-fourth and Twenty-fifth Infantry regiments first appeared in 1971, and since then it has been the standard work on the subject. Solidly researched and broad in scope, Fowler's book engages the reader with clearly written prose. Furthermore, Fowler's experience as a white officer assigned in 1952 to the black Twenty-fifth Armored Infantry Battalion—"the last surviving remnant of the once proud and honorable all black Twenty-fifth Infantry Regiment"—gave him invaluable insight into the thoughts and actions of black soldiers, who suffered constant prejudice and discrimination and still maintained an excellent record. Under similar trying circumstances, the nineteenth-century Twenty-fifth Infantry also had a record of significant achievement.

These frontier soldiers were called "buffalo soldiers," the name first being given to troopers of the Tenth Cavalry by Indian warriors during the Cheyenne War of 1867–69. Soon it was applied to the enlisted personnel of the Ninth Cavalry then campaigning on the Texas frontier, and not long thereafter, it was extended to include the men of the Twenty-fourth and Twenty-fifth Infantry regiments.

The principal criticism, and a legitimate one, of *The Black Infantry in the West* is the lack of attention to individual "buffalo soldiers." For example, Fowler mentions only two of the five soldiers from the Twenty-fourth Infantry who were awarded the Congressional Medal of Honor in the years 1874–89. Fortunately, interest in the buffalo soldiers has grown during the twenty-five years since Fowler's book first appeared. Buffalo-soldier organizations have been formed nationwide, from Florida to California and from Texas to the Canadian border, in order to promote and preserve the legacy of these black veterans. Since 1988, four television documentaries, a U.S. postage stamp, and a number of statues have appeared to honor them. In 1990 thousands attended the unveiling ceremonies at Fort Leavenworth, Kansas, of the superb statue of a mounted buffalo soldier, which included a principal address given by then Chairman of the Joint Chiefs of Staff, General Colin Powell.

In addition, the publication of many excellent regional and specialized studies has greatly expanded our knowledge of the black military experience. Readers who wish additional information on decorated soldiers can consult Preston E. Amos, *Above and Beyond in the West: Black Medal of Honor Winners, 1870–1890* (Washington, D.C.: Potomac Corral, 1974). Frank N. Schubert's first-rate *Buffalo Soldiers, Braves and Brass: The Story of Fort Robinson, Nebraska* (Shippensburg, Pa.: White Mane Publishing, 1993) contains excellent photographs and much new information on the life and times of black enlisted men on the Northern Plains. Schubert's *On the Trail of the Buffalo Soldiers: Biographies of African-Americans in the U.S. Army, 1866–1917* (Wilmington, Del.: Scholarly Resources, 1995), an invaluable biographical reference, includes entries for enlisted soldiers of the Ninth and Tenth Cavalry regiments and the Twenty-fourth and Twenty-fifth Infantry regiments. Monroe Billington, *The Buffalo Soldiers in New Mexico, 1866–1900* (Niwot: University Press of Colorado, 1991), though limited in scope, discusses both the cavalry and the infantry. My own work, *The Buffalo Soldiers: A Narrative of the Negro Cavalry in the West* (Norman: University of Oklahoma Press, 1967), contains detailed maps of campaign areas and military operations involving both cavalry and infantry units.

These publications further enrich our knowledge of the "buffalo soldiers," cavalry and infantry. In the last analysis, however, Fowler's book is still essential reading for a comprehensive understanding of the role of the black infantry on the expanding western frontier.

WILLIAM H. LECKIE

Winter Springs, Florida
February 1996

Preface

It was a hot, muggy morning in June 1952 when I reported
for duty as a second lieutenant of infantry to the First
Armored Division at Fort Hood, Texas. I was uncomfort-
able in my heavily starched khakis and more than some-
what apprehensive of the future. After my records were
processed, a major handed me a bulky manila envelope and,
with a smile on his face, announced that I was being assigned
to the "shady side of the hill." Everybody in hearing distance laughed at the major's remark. Being naive I supposed
that the Twenty-fifth Armored Infantry Battalion was one
of those lucky units at Fort Hood that had a tree or two in
its area; however, the moment I stepped into the battalion
headquarters, it was apparent that the officer at division
headquarters was attempting to be humorous in a rather
tasteless manner. The Twenty-fifth Armored Infantry
Battalion was the last surviving remnant of the once proud
and honorable all black Twenty-fifth Infantry Regiment.

My assignments as a platoon leader and later as a unit
administrator put me in direct contact with the tragic story

of the oppression of black people in white America. The frustrated hopes, shattered dreams, continued insults, denied opportunities, racist remarks, and second class treatment were all too visible and shocking as I served with those fine soldiers. My tour of duty in that battalion was an experience in human understanding and insight that I will never forget. The tragic nature of our racist society had left untold scars on the lives of those black soldiers. Yet, without rancor or noticeable bitterness, they served their country in an exemplary manner.

Several years later, my interest in the Twenty-fifth Regiment was renewed when I discovered that it and its sister regiment, the Twenty-fourth Infantry Regiment, had spent the last third of the nineteenth century on the American frontier. Their service, hardships, and contributions to the eventual pacification of the West, I discovered, was a story never before told in detail. The burden of this study is the narration of their experiences on the frontier. The story of the black infantry in the West is one in which all Americans, and especially black Americans, can point to with pride.

Acknowledgments

In the research, preparation, and writing of this book, I am deeply indebted to a number of people. The helpful assistance of Miss Sara Jackson of the National Archives is sincerely appreciated. Of special significance were the courteous assistance and the photographs given to me by the staff of the Montana State Historical Society, Helena, Montana. I am particularly indebted to Thomas Phillips of the University of Wisconsin for his invaluable help and information in the research of this manuscript. Dr. Edward Bennett and Dr. Lewis Buchanan of Washington State University were of real service to me by reading the manuscript and making many helpful comments. Special thanks and gratitude are reserved for Dr. David Stratton of the history department of the Washington State University. Professor Stratton's encouragement, time, patience, and constructive criticisms were crucial in the preparation of this manuscript.

I would be thoughtless, if I did not express my gratitude to my children Chris, Clark, Sally, and Andy who were so understanding about their father's lack of visibility around the house. Finally, I wish to state my deep appreciation to my wife Mary Jane. Her constant concern, understanding, and seemingly limitless patience made it possible for me to work undisturbed for long periods of time. In many respects this book is as much the result of her sacrifices as it is mine.

The Black Infantry
in the West
1869-1891

1

The Army
in the West

The victorious Union Army held its final grand review in Washington in May of 1865. In a parade that took two days, blue-clad regiments of cavalry and infantry marched down Pennsylvania Avenue past a reviewing stand laden with dignitaries. As the troops passed in review for the last time, their comrades in arms at hundreds of camps were stacking arms in preparation for the trip home. Over a million happy, weary, homesick volunteers were being mustered out of Mr. Lincoln's army.[1] Men who had been at Bull Run, Shiloh, Antietam, Vicksburg, Gettysburg, and hundreds of other places where men fought and died, were eagerly returning to their homes and families. In the midst of all the confusion and excitement of dismantling one of the largest armies in the world, one group of soldiers stood in place and awaited orders. That group, only 16,000 men strong, was the regular army of the United States.

The task facing the regular army in 1865 was overwhelming. It was to replace volunteer units scattered all across the nation who were clamoring to be mustered out of the service and sent home. The continued discharge of volunteers would have placed the regular army in an impossible position had not Congress intervened in July 1866 and increased the authorized strength. The regular army was ordered to occupy the vanquished South, while regulars under General Philip H. Sheridan patrolled the Mexican border in a show of force to the French and Maximilian. Then, from the West came urgent requests for troops to relieve the volunteer units, many of which by 1866 were on the verge of mutiny.[2]

To meet these needs the regular army was forced to send hastily organized, understrength regiments and companies to the critical areas. The legislation of 1866 authorized 54,304 officers and men in the regular army. However, during the period of the Indian wars, from 1866 to 1891, the actual strength of the army was approximately 25,000 men.[3] The act of 1866 also provided that officers who were in the regular army at the beginning of the Civil War were to revert to their original ranks. This meant that some wartime generals and colonels found themselves wearing captain's bars again.[4] The additional officers were selected from the volunteers and were likewise reduced in rank. A gray-haired lieutenant was not an uncommon sight in the postwar army.[5]

The officers and men of the regular army who were sent to the West faced problems of staggering proportions, one of which was the vast land area that they were responsible for protecting and pacifying. With a strength of only 25,000 men in the entire army, a shortage of troops was a constant complaint from the frontier commanders. General Philip H. Sheridan, commander of the Division of the Missouri, emphasized the problem in 1874 when he reported that in his division alone there were 99 Indian tribes numbering 192,000 persons scattered over 1,000,000 square miles of frontier country. He stated that to protect this enormous area he had only 17,819 officers and men.[6]

Four years later he again emphasized his manpower shortage for the task at hand. Sheridan pointed out that he was required to garrison seventy-three posts and protect an area of country that extended from Canada in the north to the Rio Grande in the south with a force of only 13,468 men. This averaged out, he reported, to be only one man for every 120 miles in the Department of Texas and one to every 75 square miles in the Department of Dakota. The same was true for the departments of the Platte and the Missouri. He concluded by stating, "When it is borne in mind that this immense section of country has to be under surveillance against Indians, and raiding parties from the Mexican side of the Rio Grande, the work that has to be performed by that portion of our army located within this military division will be appreciated by all military men, and by those who have ever lived upon our frontier."[7]

The most pressing problem facing the regular army in the West was the Indian wars. The Indian style of warfare was forcing the army to reexamine its current concept of operations. The Civil War had accustomed officers and soldiers to fight with massed regiments and artillery, but against Indians such tactics were impractical. The Indian engaged in a guerrilla-style warfare that relied upon deception and hit-and-run tactics. Commanders schooled to think in terms of slow moving columns and the deliberate massing of men for frontal assaults, found themselves unprepared to combat the elusive Indians. One officer serving on the Texas frontier reported that Indian warfare differed so much from what the Civil War veterans had experienced that they were ill-prepared to cope with it. For them it was "an absolutely new kind of warfare, and the experience we had to gain, and that quickly . . . was to everybody in the command of a kind we had never seen or encountered."[8]

The frontier soldier faced an enemy who was considered by many to be the best horseman in the world. The well-trained Indian pony proved a good mount to ride in combat. The Indian horse was swift and could be controlled by applying pressure with the knees, leaving both hands free to shoot a bow and arrow or rifle.[9] George Armstrong Custer, who later met his death at the hands of mounted warriors, held the horsemanship of the Plains Indian in high esteem.[10] Military historian Fairfax Downey has written concerning the Indian and his horse:

> The plains Indians, mounted on the descendants of Coronado's chargers, were termed the finest light horsemen the world ever has seen, the tactics that have never been equalled by Bedouin, Cossack, Numidan, or Tartar at his best.[11]

Walter Prescott Webb has said in his classic, *The Great Plains:*

> Thus armed, equipped, and mounted the Plains Indians were both picturesque and dangerous warriors—the red knights of the prairie. They were far better equipped for successful warfare in their own country than the white men who came against them, and presented to the European or American conqueror problems different from those found elsewhere on the continent.[12]

In addition to his skilled horsemanship, the Indian had the advantage of fighting in territory where he had lived for years.

As individuals or as a tribe, Indians were capable of enduring the hardships of long marches in all kinds of weather and under all types of conditions. His ability to move quickly and travel great distances was as useful in defensive as offensive maneuver. The famous Indian fighter of the frontier army, General George Crook, was much impressed by the tactical use the Indian made of his mobility. In his report of 1876 he noted, with a military man's appreciation, the ability of Indians to move their lodges and families at the rate of fifty miles per day with scouts out in all directions at distances of twenty to thirty miles. With this kind of tactical advantage the Indians, said Crook, could choose the time and place of battle, or avoid it altogether.[13]

It was the army's inability to inflict a decisive punishment on the elusive Indian that prompted General Sheridan to listen to a plan suggested by one of his aides in the fall of 1868. Major George A. Forsyth devised a strategy whereby the army would fight the Indian using Indian tactics. He proposed that the army enlist a small, highly mobile force of experienced frontier scouts and use Indian methods to track down the war parties. By forcing the Indians to split up into smaller isolated groups, Forsyth reasoned that he could then compel them to fight or surrender. Sheridan, disturbed by the Indians' apparent immunity to defeat, was willing to try anything to diminish their invulnerability, and gave Forsyth permission to put the plan into operation.[14]

Forsyth's command of fifty veteran frontier scouts left Fort Wallace, Kansas, in early September of 1868 in search of war parties reported to be in the vicinity. On September 17 the small unit came under attack by several hundred Indian warriors. In what was to be one of the heroic fights of the Indian campaigns, the Forsyth force was saved from total annihilation by the timely arrival of black troopers of the Tenth Cavalry eight days after the battle began. Under the circumstances, the Forsyth plan could hardly be termed a success, and the Beecher Island fight, as it was later called, closed the book on the idea of fighting Indians, Indian style.[15]

Finally, General Sheridan came up with a strategy designed to take the tactical advantage away from the Indians. The one time of year that Indians were least mobile, and therefore most vulnerable to attack, was winter. Only when snow and ice covered the ground and the Indians were resting in their winter camp could the army have a better than equal chance of · delivering a severe blow. Knowing the Indians' ponies were not in prime condition then, and that the Indians did not believe the white men capable of fighting in winter, Sheridan planned a winter expedition against the Indians near the Washita Mountains in Indian Territory. For the expedition leader, Sheridan chose an officer noted for his daring and willingness to do the unexpected, George Armstrong Custer, the Civil War "boy general." Custer, who was given command of the Seventh Cavalry for this purpose, was enthusiastic about the possibilities of a winter campaign against the Indian. He was quick to see that one of the advantages of a winter assault would be to force the Indians to fight under conditions of the army's choosing. Later Custer was to write, "A winter campaign against the Indians was certainly in accordance with that maxim in the art of war which directs one to do that which the enemy neither expects nor desires to be done. At the same time it would dispel the old-fogey idea, which was not without supporters in the army, and which was confidently relied on by the Indians themselves, that the winter season was an insurmountable barrier to the prosecution of a successful campaign."[16]

On the bitter cold morning of November 23, 1868, Custer and his column marched out of Camp Supply in Indian Territory and, in what was called the Battle of the Washita, delivered a damaging blow to the Indians of the northern plains.[17] The significance of the battle was not in terms of the casualties inflicted on the Indians, but in surmounting one of the Indians' major defenses against attack—winter weather.

As news of Custer's attack spread among the Indians, Sheridan's strategy had the desired effect. The Indians were faced with two alternatives: either they could agree to remain peaceably on the reservations, or they would have to live in a state of continual warfare against the army. If they should choose the latter course they would have to be prepared to fight a year-round war. For the next twenty-three years the army in the West was engaged in keeping the western tribes on reservations and campaigning against those who chose to fight rather than become reservation Indians.[18]

The story of the regular army on the frontier, located deep in hostile territory, is one of the fascinating chapters of American history. The frontier soldier in his forage cap and uniform of a loose, dark blue tunic with light blue trousers, was as much a part of the development of the West as the fur trapper, miner, cattleman, or farmer. He was not a parade ground soldier but a professional who adapted to unconventional warfare in a country that was as harsh as it was beautiful. It was a rugged group of men who occupied the forts that dotted the landscape of the West. Arranged in the shape of a square, most frontier posts were crudely constructed and equipped with a minimum of conveniences. Officers' quarters were always inadequate and the enlisted men's barracks were generally in a state of disrepair. Most of the buildings were constructed from logs, roughhewn lumber, or adobe, and were cold in the winter and hot in the summer.[19]

The depressive nature of the living conditions was not eased by a bountiful or varied menu at the mess hall. Frontier army rations did not include such items as milk, eggs, butter, or fresh vegetables. Only the basic items, flour, bacon, lard, hardtack, coffee, and other staples were issued by the commissary, and even these were often slow to reach the forts and unpredictable as to amount and quality. Most enlisted men spent a large portion of their pay on food purchased from the post traders to add variety to their diets.[20] Many posts maintained a garden in which men were detailed to raise vegetables for use in the mess hall. Some fortunate garrisons had farmers nearby with whom it was possible to barter for fresh milk and eggs; but, if the diet was poor in garrisons, it was miserable in the field. When on extended patrols, expeditions, or long details, the usual bill of fare in the field was hardtack, bacon, and coffee. It was not uncommon for men at frontier posts to suffer from scurvy because of inadequate diets.[21]

Contrary to fictional accounts of the frontier army, monotony and boredom characterized the life of the enlisted man at western posts. The frontier forts were invariably isolated from civilization and few social contacts were provided for the officers and men.[22] With minimal recreational opportunities the men eagerly looked forward to any activity that would take them away from the post and relieve the monotony of garrison life. Many officers and men spent over twenty years on the frontier without an assignment near populated areas.

If monotony and boredom were the experience of most frontier soldiers, it was even more the case for those assigned to the infantry regiments. Since the army had to use mounted troops to meet and engage a mounted enemy, most of the fighting was done by the cavalry. Consequently, nearly all accounts of the Indian wars, both fictional and factual, devote their attention to the cavalry. Nevertheless, there were more infantry regiments stationed in the West than there were calvary.[23] The infantry's principal military responsibility was guarding and maintaining the post, in addition to providing escort for government supply trains, railroad construction crews, or army paymasters. Many infantry companies engaged in the construction of telegraph lines between frontier forts and wagon roads connecting posts to nearby communities. On numerous occasions the infantry encountered hostile Indians while performing its duties; for the most part, however, the infantryman's job was unglamorous hard work performed in isolated and lonely places. Standing guard at a wilderness water hole, walking beside a slow plodding wagon train over hundreds of hot and dusty miles, and digging holes in sunbaked soil for telegraph poles was not the picture of adventure and excitement portrayed by most stories about the army in the West. Perhaps that is why the story of the frontier army infantry has been long neglected. Unglamorous as it was, the infantryman's contribution to the pacification and protection of the West was as important as that of the cavalryman.

Two frontier infantry units are of particular interest, partly because of their notable records of service, but also because they represented a new addition to the composition of the regular army. In the post-Civil War years the Twenty-fourth and Twenty-fifth Infantry Regiments garrisoned several isolated frontier army posts. Both regiments were made up of black troops.

The use of black troops in the army had from the beginning of the Civil War been a controversial issue. At the outset of the war blacks offering their services as Union soldiers were met with a steadfast refusal—it was considered a "white man's war."[24] In spite of the Lincoln administration's indifference, black leaders and the abolitionists continued to urge black men to enlist in the Union Army. It was thought that if black men were given the opportunity to serve and fulfill a patriotic service, they would stand a better chance of being accepted as first-class citizens. Frederick Douglass suggested:

> Once let the black man get upon his person the brass letters, U.S., let him get an eagle on his button, and a musket on his shoulder and bullets in his pocket, and there is no power on earth which can deny that he has earned the right to citizenship in the United States.[25]

Not until white enlistments began to drop, however, did the Lincoln administration agree to consider the use of black soldiers. On July 17, 1862 Congress passed legislation giving black men the opportunity to join the Union Army.[26] Even as Congress took these steps there were those who voiced opposition to the use of black soldiers. Many people in the North believed that blacks, especially ex-slaves, were too ignorant and cowardly to make good soldiers.[27] As it turned out, black soldiers in the Civil War not only won a place of honor for themselves but proved their manhood by their courage and tenacity in battle. In enemy encounters at Petersburg, Port Hudson, and Nashville, black soldiers proved to be as brave and as well-disciplined as white troops. General Benjamin F. Butler, with nine regiments of black infantry, stormed New Market Heights in September 1864 and wrested the fortifications from the Confederate forces at the cost of 1,000 men. Butler later said that as he rode among his cheering black troops at New Market Heights, he "felt in [his] inmost heart that the capacity of the negro race for soldiers had then and there been fully settled forever."[28]

The most historically significant change in the composition of the regular army in the post-Civil War period was the enlistment of black soldiers. In the legislation of 1866 provisions were made for six regiments of black troops in the regular army: two were to be cavalry and four infantry. The black cavalry regiments, the Ninth and Tenth, scored two of the finest records of all the cavalry units in the Indian wars.[29] Originally the four infantry regiments were split up, with two staying on duty in the South and the other two moving to the frontier.[30] In March 1869 Congress passed an army reorganization bill which provided for the consolidation of the four black infantry regiments into two. The two regiments in the South were sent to Louisiana, consolidated there, and given the designation of the Twenty-fifth Infantry, while the remaining two infantry regiments were consolidated in Texas and designated the Twenty-fourth Infantry.

The following year the Twenty-fifth Infantry was ordered to join the Twenty-fourth Infantry and occupy the posts protecting the southwestern edge of the Texas frontier. The two black infantry regiments spent the next twenty-two years as a part of the regular army's thin blue line attempting to bring peace to the troubled western frontier.

NOTES

1. William A. Ganoe, *The History of the United States Army*, p. 305.

2. Russell F. Weigley, *History of the United States Army*, p. 266; Fairfax Downey, *Indian-Fighting Army*, p. 20.

3. Weigley, *History of the Army*, p. 267. The regular army was consistently below its authorized strength because of the lack of congressional appropriations. On March 3, 1869 Congress reduced the authorized number of regiments in the army from forty-five to twenty-five.

4. Ibid., p. 267.

5. Downey, *Indian-Fighting Army*, p. 20.

6. U.S., Congress, House Executive Documents, *Annual Report of the Secretary of War, 1874–1875*, 43rd Cong., 2d Sess., I, 22–23.

7. U.S., Congress, House Executive Documents, *Annual Report of the Secretary of War, 1878–1879*, 45th Cong., 3d Sess., II, 33.

8. Captain R. G. Carter, *On the Border with Mackenzie*, p. 536, cited by Oliver Knight, *Following the Indian Wars*, pp. 15–16.

9. Walker D. Wyman, *The Wild Horse of the West*, pp. 78–79.

10. P. E. Byrne, *Soldiers on the Plains*, p. 178.

11. Downey, *Indian-Fighting Army*, p. 19.

12. Walter Prescott Webb, *The Great Plains*, p. 68. A

view that suggests the Indians were not great warriors on horseback is found in Frank Gilbert Roe, *The Indian and The Horse*, pp. 219–246.

13. U.S., Congress, House Executive Documents, *Annual Report of the Secretary of War, 1876–1877*, 44th Cong., 2d Sess., I, 500.

14. John Tebbel, *The Compact History of the Indian Wars*, pp. 239–240.

15. James Hutchins, "The Fight at Beecher Island," ed., B. W. Allred, J. C. Dykes, Frank Goodwyn, and D. Harper Sims, *Great Western Indian Fights*, pp. 163–174.

16. George Armstrong Custer, *My Life on the Plains*, pp. 139–140.

17. Lawrence Frost, "Battle of the Washita," in *Great Western Indian Fights*, pp. 175–181; Ralph K. Andrist, *The Long Death: The Last Days of the Plains Indians* (New York: The Macmillan Company, 1964), pp. 154–162; Byrne, *Soldiers of the Plains*, pp. 143–154; Downey, *Indian-Fighting Army*, pp. 70–83.

18. Tebbel, *The Compact History of the Indians Wars*, p. 281.

19. U.S., Congress, House Executive Documents, *Annual Report of the Secretary of War, 1869–1870*, 41st Cong., 2d Sess., I, 31.

20. Don Rickey, Jr., *Forty Miles A Day on Beans and Hay*, pp. 116–122; William M. Hoge, Jr., "The Logistical System of the U.S. Army During the Indian Wars, 1866–1889," pp. 16–19.

21. William H. Leckie, *The Buffalo Soldiers*, p. 44; Hoge, "The Logistical System of the Army," pp. 15–16; Rickey, *Forty Miles on Beans and Hay*, pp. 131–132.

22. Rickey, *Forty Miles on Beans and Hay*, p. 88.

23. *Annual Report of the Secretary of War, 1869–1870*, p. 24.

24. M. A. DeWolfe Howe, ed., *Home Letters of General Sherman*, p. 252; James M. McPherson, *The Negro's Civil War*, p. 161.

25. *Douglass' Monthly*, V (August, 1863), 852, quoted in McPherson, *The Negro's Civil War*, p. 161. An excellent study of the black soldier in the Civil War is provided by Dudley T.

Cornish, *The Sable Arm*. A classic account of a black regiment in the Union Army, written by its commanding officer, is Thomas Wentworth Higginson's *Army Life in a Black Regiment*.

26. Cornish, *The Sable Arm*, pp. 34–47; McPherson, *The Negro's Civil War*, p. 165.

27. McPherson, *The Negro's Civil War*, p. 164; See also Cornish, *The Sable Arm*, Foreword and pp. 1–10; and Roy P. Basler, ed., *The Collected Works of Abraham Lincoln* (9 Vols., New Brunswick, New Jersey, 1953), VI, 90n; Bell I. Wiley, *The Life of Billy Yank*, 109–123.

28. Quoted in Cornish, *The Sable Arm*, p. 280.

29. Leckie, *The Buffalo Soldiers*, is a comprehensive study of the black cavalry in the Indian wars.

30. The original four black infantry regiments were designated as the Thirty-eighth, Thirty-ninth, Fortieth, and Forty-first Infantry. The Thirty-ninth and Fortieth Infantry remained in the South and the Thirty-eighth and Forty-first were sent to the West. The War Department in 1869 consolidated the Thirty-eighth and Forty-first into the Twenty-fourth Infantry and the Thirty-ninth and Fortieth into the Twenty-fifth Infantry. U.S., Congress, House Executive Documents, *Annual Report of the Secretary of War, 1869–1870*, 41st Cong., 2d Sess., I, 96–99.

2

The

Texas Years

The transfer of the Fortieth Infantry Regiment to Louisiana gave rise to an incident that was indicative of the prejudice many in the army had against black troops. Normally, when regiments were moved by train they were put on passenger cars. But when, on March 31, 1869, the Fortieth Infantry marched into the railroad station at Goldsboro, North Carolina, they found cattle cars and freight cars waiting to take them on board. The regiment spent a total of ten days in such cars en route to New Orleans. Upon arrival the officer in charge of the regiment lodged a complaint against the Quartermaster General, charging him with discrimination. The Quartermaster General replied by suggesting that the officer in charge had been at fault for accepting substandard transportation.[1]

Within a few days after its arrival at New Orleans, the Fortieth Infantry was consolidated with the Thirty-ninth Infantry and designated as the Twenty-fifth Infantry Regiment. The regiment was less than a day old when it was pressed into service on behalf of maintaining law and order. At the request of Governor H. C. Warmoth, a company of the regiment was sent to Opelousas, Louisiana to help preserve the peace in that community.[2] During its brief stay in unreconstructed Louisiana, the Twenty-fifth was frequently used by civil authorities to assist in maintaining order in cities where civil disturbances erupted.

While the Twenty-fifth Infantry was beginning its career in Louisiana, the Twenty-fourth Infantry Regiment was taking shape at Fort McKavitt, Texas. The Thirty-eighth Infantry Regiment had marched from New Mexico across Texas to consolidate with the Forty-first Infantry. The latter regiments were both experienced units with nearly three years of frontier service behind them. The Thirty-eighth had fought in a number of Indian engagements in the West;[3] and in the summer of 1867 a company of the Thirty-eighth had assisted in the defense of Fort Wallace, Kansas, against a Cheyenne attack led by Chief Roman Nose. General Custer's wife recorded an account of the battle and particularly of the part played by the men of the Thirty-eighth.

> The post had been so short of men that a dozen negro soldiers, who had come with their wagon from an outpost for supplies, were placed near the garrison on picket duty. While the fight was going on, the two officers in command found themselves near each other on the skirmish-line, and observed a wagon with four mules tearing out to the line of battle. It was filled with negroes, standing up, all firing in the direction of the Indians. The driver lashed the mules with his black snake, and roared at them as they ran. When the skirmish-line was reached, the colored men leaped out and began firing again. No one had ordered them to leave their picket-station, but they were determined that no soldiering should be carried on in which their valor was not proved.[4]

The Forty-first Infantry had been stationed along the Rio Grande River since it was organized. Nearly all the men recruited into the regiment were unskilled and uneducated. But the commanding officer, "by discipline and constant work made it one of the crack regiments of the army during the . . . years . . . it was at various posts on the Texas frontier."[5]

In June 1870 the various companies of the Twenty-fifth Infantry were ordered to leave Louisiana and rendezvous at San Antonio, Texas. In San Antonio the regiment was given ten days to rest and refit before joining the Twenty-fourth Infantry on the Texas frontier. A special inspection of the Twenty-fifth was made on June 20 by the acting Assistant Inspector General of the Department of Texas. He reported that it was a good infantry regiment with an excellent health record and noted for low desertions. In his report, however, he called attention to a problem common to all black units: the added time and labor put upon officers in the black regiments by having them keep all books themselves, and make out all rolls, returns, and accounts. Because of the lack of formal education among the black troops, he suggested that an educated clerk be hired to do all the bookkeeping as well as teach the men to read and write. He concluded by saying, "In this way too the negroes who serve in the army will become intelligent and be so much better fitted to take their places as the political equals of white men, which they have become, under the Constitution. This is a matter of grave importance, and in my judgment should be called to the attention of the highest authority."[6] Eventually, a solution to this problem evolved within the organization of the black regiments which was destined to make a significant contribution to the development of the educational program of the army.[7]

The black infantry regiments began a tour of duty in Texas in August 1870 that lasted over a decade. They were garrisoned in frontier forts that bordered the Staked Plains on the west and the Rio Grande River on the south and southwest. The Twenty-fourth was headquartered at Fort McKavitt with its companies stationed at Forts Bliss, Clark, Davis, Duncan, Quitman, and Stockton with headquarters at Fort Davis.[8] Through the hardships they endured, the duties they performed, and the competence of their officers, the Twenty-fourth and Twenty-fifth Infantry were molded into two of the army's most outstanding regiments.

Throughout the Texas years attempts were made to have the black regiments disbanded or consolidated.[9] Prejudice against black men in uniform was still current among some officers of the army. As early as 1870, Colonel J. J. Reynolds, the commander of the Department of Texas, recommended that the black infantry be consolidated into one regiment.

> The terms of enlistment of the men of the Twenty-fourth Infantry are rapidly expiring and scarcely any are reenlisting. The Twenty-fifth will, on the first of June next, contain about 550 men.
>
> It does not appear probable from our experience thus far that both these regiments can be kept up to an efficient standard with colored men. I have the honor therefore respectfully to recommend that they be consolidated into one regiment, and that the other regiment be filled up with white men.
>
> This would prove a measure of efficiency and economy; the officers of one regiment can command the consolidated regiment to occupy the Posts now garrisoned by the Twenty-fourth and the officers of the other regiment would be available to recruit a new regiment.[10]

This recommendation was forwarded through military channels and eventually was placed in the hands of President Ulysses S. Grant. Because there were indications that recruiting officers were not enthusiastic enough in seeking black recruits, President Grant ordered that renewed efforts be made to enlist black men to fill the two regiments.[11]

Army service on the frontier of Texas was not an easy duty. For the enlisted men it meant long hours, hard work, and the usual low pay. The task of defending posts against Indian depredations was complicated by the vast distances, which spread the regiments across a single narrow line along the frontier. The commander of the Department of Texas in his annual report commented that the service of the troops in his command had been very difficult. They were required, he reported, to protect the frontier against Indians over a distance of about 1,300 miles. In addition his command was responsible for patrolling 400 miles of the Rio Grande against marauders and bandits.[12] He also stated that the troop shortage was not helped by the extra duties assigned the men. To enlist a man as a soldier and then use him as a laborer, he declared, was neither efficient nor conducive to an effective military force.[13]

Nor was the enlisted man of the frontier army compensated for his long hours and hard work with pleasant living quarters. Most of the Texas frontier posts had been constructed prior to the Civil War, and due to poor maintenance, they were in a state of disrepair. Colonel Edmund Shriver, who made an inspection of all these posts in 1872, described the conditions at Fort Clark—considered one of the better posts—in these terms:

> The quarters are wretchedly [constructed] and therefore nothing beyond shelter and ordinary police can reasonably be looked for. All except two companies of cavalry are in huts. . . . This is the proper place to remark on the utter inadequacy of decent quarters for officers also, and of the absence of an administrative building for offices. The guard

house is cramped; the regimental Adjutant's office is in a tent. There is no place for divine service or instruction. There is no proper room in which to hold courts-martial. There are no places for servants, they and the laundresses living in miserable shanties. The public stores are imperfectly covered with paulins or put in insecure huts, improvised at great expense, of perishable paulins, liable to be stolen, injured etc. The necessity for assembling at a Post troops in such numbers that they cannot be decently sheltered should be imperative; when it is, no time should be lost in making the necessary provision for them. It is least expensive in the end, and it is the right of a garrison, officers and men.[14]

Living conditions in the succeeding years did not improve measurably for the Twenty-fourth and Twenty-fifth, since only limited funds were allotted by the War Department for the repair or construction of quarters. Some men in the black infantry in Texas had not for several years slept one night under a substantial roof. In 1875 the regimental commander of the Twenty-fifth complained to the Department of Texas about the lack of proper quarters for his men, telling them that in the six years that the Twenty-fifth Infantry had been in Texas the band and noncommissioned officer staff had not spent one day in proper quarters. For two years, in both summer and winter, they were quartered in tents at Fort Clark. At Fort Davis they were drowned out after every heavy rain. Such conditions, he reported, were far from satisfactory for troop morale. "I have visited the band quarters several times during the past summer to find everything saturated with rain, the dirt floor full four inches deep of mud, and the men sitting at meals while their heads and backs were being defiled with ooze from the dripping dirt roof."[15] Andrews concluded his remarks by stating that the poor living conditions were the reason many men were not re-enlisting. He urged that immediate steps be taken to improve the barracks in his regiment.[16]

To make matters even worse, conditions within the enlisted men's quarters were no better. The double bunks were often made of crude cottonwood poles with a rough board bottom and mattresses consisting of bedsacks filled monthly with fresh hay. Low ceilings prohibited the circulation of air in summer or winter.[17] One inspector noted in his report that recent rains which had soaked the roof of an infantry barracks, made the quarters little better than a mud hole. The men had patched up the holes in the roof with tarps, blankets, and ponchos because no repairs on the adobe barracks could be made until the sun came out and dried the mud.[18]

Under such primitive and cheerless conditions the enlisted men welcomed any opportunity to escape from the dreary routine of garrison life. They looked forward to escort and scout duty, even when it sent them deep into hostile Indian territory, because it afforded them a chance to get away from the post. The effects of the isolation on the men impelled one regimental chaplain to observe that the location of Fort Davis in a vast uninhabited country and the lack of any creative diversions, "tends to superinduce a restive spirit, and creates a cheerless atmosphere— which render temptations to intemperance very strong."[19] A post commander of Fort Davis in 1872 described the situation in more expansive terms:

> Nearest telegraph and railroad station, Austin, Texas, distance of 450 miles. Post Office at the Post. Nearest town of any importance is Franklin, opposite El Paso, Mexico, distance 225 miles. There is a small settlement on the Rio Grande opposite Del Porte, Mexico, distance from the Post, 90 miles. Good wagon roads to San Antonio via Fort Clark or Fort Concho, distance 466 miles. Wagon road to Fort Quitman, distance 145 miles. There is a small

settlement of about 150 Mexicans and 25 Americans at the Post mostly dependent upon the Post for their support and therefore not permanent residents.[20]

It was the fate of the black infantry regiments to serve most of their army careers at such isolated frontier posts.

Since Indian fighting was primarily a cavalryman's war, the infantry troops did not participate in combat with the Indians as frequently as their black comrades in the cavalry. As a result, the cavalry was freed from most garrison duties so that it could move to the field on short notice. It fell to the infantry to do the lion's share of fatigue and housekeeping chores on the frontier posts. On occasion infantry detachments conducted scouting patrols if there was a lack of cavalry units, but most of the time they were engaged in routine assignments.

Infantry duty on the Texas frontier in 1870 meant performing a variety of jobs. For example, at Fort Duncan in 1870, in addition to the usual guard and fatigue details, the infantry companies were engaged in escort duty, scouting patrols, barracks construction, and repair of quarters.[21] Most of the infantry units stationed at Texas posts found it necessary to detail men for the job of making their quarters livable. This kind of work was complicated by the fact that a large number of the men in the black infantry were unskilled and inexperienced in the use of tools.[22] Escort duty, the most frequent off-post assignment, meant traveling hundreds of miles as guards for government supply trains, contract trains, and survey parties. An escort was fulfilled by Company C of the Twenty-fifth in 1875 in which the unit was attached to a wagon train that left Fort Sill in Indian Territory on March 26, and arrived at Fort Stockton, Texas, twenty-nine days and 490 miles later.[23]

Usually when the black infantrymen were called upon to discharge scouting duties, they were mounted. Also, the cavalry was often augmented by mounted infantry troops to fill the need for scouting patrols. These patrols were often in the field for a month at a time and covered large areas of territory. One scouting party, a detachment of mounted black infantry and cavalry, left Fort Davis on October 5, 1871, and during the twenty-nine days that it was absent from the post traveled 500 miles across Indian country.[24] On large scouting expeditions on the Texas frontier the use of infantry as camp and supply train guards was standard operating procedure and the field orders usually spelled out this specific responsibility.[25]

An off-post assignment that tested the strength and stamina of the men of the black infantry was the road building and repair detail which called upon them to construct military wagon roads between frontier posts and neighboring communities. In many instances companies were sent on road building projects for several months at a time. Company B of the Twenty-fourth was engaged in constructing a road between San Felipe, Texas, and Fort Davis from September 26, 1879 until January 29, 1880. During those cold and rainy months in the field not one man was reported sick until the company returned to post.[26] Such a record bears witness to the endurance and character of the frontier black soldiers.

High on the list of priorities in the Department of Texas was the construction of military telegraph lines. Beginning in 1870 department commanders had advocated linking all frontier posts to their headquarters by telegraph, since rapid communication was necessary for efficient and effective military operations.[27] The job of erecting the poles and stringing the wire was assigned to the infantry and some companies were in the field for weeks and even months at a time engaged in this task.[28] Field duty of this type was hard and monotonous work, but it was not without significance in the pacification of the Texas frontier.

In earlier days, the army had posted a platoon or a company of soldiers at remount stations on the Texas frontier to provide protection and escort for the stagecoach lines. During the Civil War this service was abandoned, but after the war the stage companies again requested guards for their remount stations. Due to the shortage of troops only two or three men were detailed at each station, and this responsibility went to the infantry. Located along the roads between frontier communities and forts, the stations were usually small adobe huts or crude wooden houses with a corral and feed lot adjoining.[29]

Duty as station guards was generally a quiet, peaceful assignment, and in that respect it was appreciated by the men. It afforded an escape from the tedium of garrison life. Danger arose from the fact that the horses kept at the remount stations might tempt a band of marauding Indians to make a raid. Central Station, Texas, near Fort Stockton was the scene of such a raid which Sergeant Benjamin Stow of the Twenty-fifth Infantry described in this way:

> I have the honor to report that yesterday afternoon about 3 o'clock, I saw a party of men coming down the hill towards the station. Thinking they were cattle men I paid but little attention to them until I saw them take an old horse which was picketed about three hundred (300) yards from the station. They then advanced towards the station, and I discovered they were Indians. At the same time I saw a large party on the hill, with a herd of about forty or fifty horses and mules. I had three men besides myself together with the stage driver; and we went out about fifty yards from the station, fearing to go any further lest we should be cut off. After firing about ten minutes, they went off and then came back, we drove them off again, when they were

joined by the party from the hill, and all went off towards the Pecos River. There were fifteen in the party attacking the station. . . . I know of no loss on either side.[30]

At the end of their tour of duty as station guards the men returned to post on the next inbound stage. A source of friction between the army and the stage companies was the discriminatory practice of leaving the off-duty black station guards behind when the coach held white passengers. When unable to ride the stagecoach, the soldiers were forced to walk back to their posts, which in most cases were several miles away. In one such instance Lieutenant Colonel William R. Shafter complained to the El Paso Mail Lines about a station keeper at Leon Hole, Texas, who refused to provide either food or shelter for station guards who were left behind by the stage. He informed the company that when the black guards were put off the stage, they were obliged to walk to Fort Stockton, obtaining their rations "by their wits." Shafter concluded his letter with a warning to the company:

> I shall be glad to furnish mail escorts as long as they are wanted, but they must be properly treated. They should either be fed by the company or allowed facilities at the stations for cooking their own rations and a decent place to stay while at the station and invariably brought back by the first return stage.[31]

There was also evidence that some of the station guards received abusive treatment from stage company employees and the black infantrymen did not always remain passive in the face of such offensive acts. On one occasion an energetic and aggressive sergeant of the Twenty-fifth Infantry refused to accept insults from the stationmaster at El Muerto station and, instead, placed the man under arrest. He then notified the post commander at Fort Davis of the arrest and requested instructions. The commanding officer assured the sergeant that he approved of his actions, but because of the lack of proper jail facilities he was to release the stationmaster. The officer also stated that if in the future any employee of the stage line insults, maltreats, or abuses one of the black soldiers, the sergeant was to report it immediately. He then added, "You will be careful hereafter not to come in conflict with the stage men if it can be avoided, but at the same time you will see that the soldiers are properly treated, . . . the escorts and station guards furnished by the Government are hereby ordered not to put up with any abuse from the stage men."[32] As a result of the stationmaster's arrest the stage company was forced to investigate the incident and take corrective action.

The primary function of the stagecoach lines in Texas was to deliver mail and freight, since the Texas frontier was one of the principal mail routes between East and West. Prior to the Civil War the Butterfield Overland Mail Company had operated a mail and freight line between Tipton, Missouri and San Francisco, and many of the forts on the Texas frontier were along the route of that line.[33] After the war various independent companies operated portions of the old Butterfield route. Before the railroads forced the stagecoaches off the prairie, it was one of the most colorful and dangerous businesses in the West. The standard stagecoach seated nine persons inside and several top riders and was drawn by teams of horses or mules. Team changes were made at remount stations located approximately every twelve to sixteen miles along the route. These rugged coaches bounded along over rough roads, forded rivers, climbed mountain passes, and sped through Indian country in a race against time.[34]

Stagecoaches were frequently the target of Indian raiders or Mexican marauders. When a coach was reported overdue a detail of army troops was sent to investigate and frequently they found tragic evidence of the brutality of frontier life. On October 26, 1877, a sergeant and seven men of the Twenty-fifth were sent from Fort Stockton to look for an overdue mail stage: a few hours later they found the coach fifteen miles east of Pecos station and three-quarters of a mile from the road. Near the coach lay the body of the murdered driver with the mail and express plundered and the remnants scattered, the mules were gone and parts of the stagecoach had been removed. The detail gathered up all that was worth saving and brought it back to the post after burying the driver where they found him.[35]

As a result of such tragic incidents the stage companies demanded more army escorts for their mail lines. Because of the small manpower authorizations fixed by Congress, the army was doing extra duty in an effort to meet the demands already made upon it. Many officers believed that the stagecoach escort service was unnecessary and was only perpetuated for the convenience of the drivers who liked to have someone to talk to, to hold the reins at stops, and help out in case of an accident.[36] Colonel George L. Andrews of the Twenty-fifth Infantry said that he was commanding an understrength regiment and could not see the value of escort riders and station guards doing a job that he considered the responsibility of the contracting lines.[37]

As the number of Indian raids along the Texas frontier increased in the spring and summer of 1875, there was an outcry for more protection from the army. The increased demand placed the understrength infantry and cavalry units under a great strain, making it impossible for garrisons to provide enough men for normal fatigue details. Some settlers accused the army of inefficiency in the use of its troops. One Texan sent a complaint against Colonel Andrews to the Department of Texas stating that he held six companies of infantry in idleness while the settlers in the area lived in fear of Indian attack. In reply to the accusation, Andrews recounted the problems frontier commanders faced when confronted with many responsibilities and only a few troops to meet them. Because of the shortage of men, he stated that his troops were overworked and his post undermanned. So often were his companies in the field that it was difficult to find men enough to perform the necessary fatigue details at the post. His report enumerated all the duties his troops were called upon to perform and he concluded that he could not agree that his men were under any circumstances standing idle.[38] The demands made upon Colonel Andrews and his men at Fort Davis were repeated at the other frontier posts where the Twenty-fourth and Twenty-fifth were stationed.

In the Indian attacks of the 1870s, the Kiowas and Comanches invaded west Texas from the Red River to the Rio Grande, while the ruthless Lipans and Kickapoos raided the south from across the border. In addition to the Indian marauders there were bands of Mexicans, renegade whites, and the iniquitous *commancheros*. As the depredations continued, the army with its limited manpower sought to devise a strategy in which it could more effectively utilize its troops. In addition to the four black infantry and cavalry regiments there were usually three regiments of white troops in the Department of Texas. General C. C. Augur, commander of the Department of Texas, planned to arrange the frontier troops in a way that would provide for a continuous line of patrols. He had noted that the Texas frontier settlements which suffered most from hostile Indian incursions were those on the north, on a line extending 400 miles from Fort Richardson by way of Forts Griffin and Concho, towards Fort Stockton to the Pecos River. Settlements on the west down the Pecos and Rio Grande Rivers as far as Fort McIntosh had also been subjected to frequent raids.[39] Augur's plan was to assign parts of the frontier to each post commander, with the segments linked to form a continuous line of patrols. Garrisons such as Fort Quitman, which had only two companies of black infantry, found this operation an additional burden on their overworked troops. The official reports of the black infantry regiments for 1872 indicate that troops were out on patrol the year round with some detachments scouting as much as 100 miles on foot.[40]

While the department commanders in the West were preoccupied with the problem of local strategy, the army, with the cooperation of the Indian Bureau, was developing a larger Indian containment policy. The army was advocating a policy that would facilitate the operations of its field commanders to deal with hostile Indians who refused to stay on their reservations. In 1874 the United States government instituted a policy of enrolling all Indian tribes on the reservations, so that it would be easier to identify those Indians who were still hostile to reservation life. One unit of the black infantry was directly involved in the program. Captain Gaines Lawson and Company I of the Twenty-fifth Infantry were sent from Fort Sill, Indian Territory, to the Wichita Indian Agency at Anadarko to aid in the enrollment of the friendly Indians. Company I had been detailed to assist the Tenth Cavalry in patrolling the boundaries of Indian territory since the spring of 1872. In August the situation at the Wichita Agency became increasingly tense with the arrival of a number of unenrolled Indians. Captain Lawson, alarmed at the Indian unrest, requested reinforcements from Lieutenant Colonel John W. Davidson of the Tenth Cavalry.[41] Davidson left Fort Sill with four companies of cavalry and when he arrived at the Wichita Agency he found it crowded with Indians.

One chief, Red Food, of the Nokonis, was camped at the agency but had not enrolled with the other Indians. Davidson told the chief that he must turn in his weapons and go with him to Fort Sill as a prisoner of war. After some discussion Chief Red Food agreed to Davidson's demands and the colonel detailed his regimental adjutant and forty men to accompany the chief to his camp some 200 yards away. Upon arrival at the camp, Red Food began to balk at giving up his weapons and becoming a prisoner of war. Davidson later stated that he considered the argument at the camp only a ruse to gain time. In the midst of the discussion Red Food gave a yell, broke from the guard, and fled amidst a volley of rifle fire. Lawson had been instructed that if he heard gunfire he was to deploy his infantry company near the agency sawmill and cut off any Indians attempting to retreat up the Washita River. Company I responded as ordered and turned back the Nokonis, forcing them up the high hills bordering the river. As Davidson began to move in on the Nokonis camp, he received fire to his rear from Indians behind the commissary. They were later identified as Kiowas who were led by the outlaw Lone Wolf.

The presence of many friendly Indians complicated the situation and forced Davidson to move his cavalry units into the timber along the river and reorganize his men. Under the circumstances, he elected to dismount his men and fight on foot. The battle continued throughout the day and into the early evening hours. Sunday morning dawned with the Indians gathering for another attack on a trader's store which was situated on the high bluffs overlooking the agency. As Captain Lawson and his black infantry were moving out to reinforce the store, Davidson ordered three companies up the western slope of the bluffs to drive off the Indians, estimated to number from 200 to 300 warriors. The Indians, in a desperate maneuver to dislodge the soldiers from the store, set fire to the grass in a high wind in an attempt to burn them out. Lawson and his men moved quickly to oppose the tactic by starting counter fires. The battle continued until nightfall when the Indians withdrew from the agency.

Army casualties for the two days of fighting were four

men wounded and six horses shot. It was reported that four-
teen Indians were shot off their horses and four Indian ponies
were killed.[42] In this, as in other engagements with the
Twenty-fourth and Twenty-fifth Infantry, the Indians
found in the black infantryman an able opponent.

The fight at the Wichita Agency created new problems for the rebellious Indians. No longer would they be
able to depend upon the reservation as a sanctuary from
the army. When news of the Anadarko fight spread, many
of the hostile Indians moved away from the reservation.
Bands of renegades fled to the nearby plains in search of
a new sanctuary while the unfriendly Kiowas and Comanches retreated to the Staked Plains of west Texas.[43]

The next assignment for the army in Texas was to
bring the renegade Indians back to the reservations, a goal
that was to occupy the time and energies of the men of
the frontier garrisons for several years. One notable effort
was made in May, 1875 under the command of Lieutenant
Colonel William R. Shafter, who in later years was the
famed "rotund general" of the Spanish-American War. The
Department of Texas ordered an expedition formed for the
purpose of clearing the Staked Plains of all hostile Indians.
Except for the officers and the Seminole scouts, the entire
command was composed of black soldiers. Shafter was assigned five companies of the Tenth Cavalry, two companies from the Twenty-fourth Infantry, and one company from the Twenty-fifth Infantry. The expedition ren-
dezvoused at Fort Concho on June 20 with a supply train
of sixty-five mules and a pack train of several hundred
mules. The command left Fort Concho on July 14 with
four months' supply of rations and remained in the field
until November, when it was ordered to return to Fort
Duncan.[44] The results of this expedition provided a significant milestone in the history of the army on the Texas
frontier. A command of black soldiers had not only tra-
versed the entire area of the Staked Plains, but they had

taken an important sanctuary away from the Indians. Although Shafter and his men killed only one Indian and captured five others, they did sweep the Plains clear of all hostiles. A particularly important result of the expedition was to dispel some of the myths and fears surrounding the mysterious Staked Plains.[45]

As a matter of fact, the Twenty-fourth and Twenty-fifth infantries took part in most of the historic military expeditions on the Texas frontier from 1870 to 1880, yet seldom is their contribution noted by historians. Nor did they at that time receive official recognition for their service. One exception was the 1874 annual report of General Augur, commander of the Department of Texas, wherein he called attention to the good morale and spirit of the black regiments and their officers.[46] In fact, it seems that the black infantry regiments had an esprit de corps that was often missing in white regiments.

While the regiments in the interior of Texas were occupied in keeping renegade Indians at bay, their comrades on the Mexican border were kept busy tracking down raiders. For several years the Indians who lived in the mountains of Coahuila and Chihuahua in Mexico launched raids across the Rio Grande River into Texas. Besides the Indians, bands of cattle thieves found rustling across the border profitable and, in this, they were in many instances aided by corrupt Mexican authorities.[47] The Texas legislature requested Congress to send additional regiments to protect the border since American citizens living near the border repeatedly petitioned the United States government for protection, especially because the raids were often accompanied by killings and kidnappings.[48]

Despite American requests for the Mexican government to cooperate in punishing the raiders, the Mexican authorities were unable, and in some instances unwilling, to cope with the problem. With its understrength regiments spread along a thousand-mile border, the army's position in the matter was a difficult one, especially since their patrols were forbidden to cross the river. After many fruitless efforts to secure Mexican cooperation the army was put in the position of having to initiate a policy of hot pursuit of raiders across the border. While officially the United States government did not sanction these border incursions, unofficially such actions were given tacit approval.[49]

This was the situation in May 1873, when Colonel Ranald S. MacKenzie of the Fourth Cavalry received word that a fresh trail left by raiders had been discovered near the Rio Grande River. Mackenzie immediately sent six companies of cavalry and a detachment of the Twenty-fourth Infantry in pursuit. The command crossed the border near the Santa Rosa Mountains and rode into Mexico. On the morning of May 18 Mackenzie led a charge into a camp of Kickapoos and Lipans, killing nineteen warriors and a Lipan chief, and capturing forty women and children along with sixty-five ponies. The camp was completely destroyed along with all the stores and supplies left by the Indians.[50] Although Mackenzie's raid was a shock to both the Mexicans and Indians, it was not impressive enough to stop the raids which continued all along the border.[51]

In 1877 Lieutenant Colonel Shafter and the Twenty-fourth Infantry were involved in another border crossing, this time to rescue two Mexican guides who had been taken captive by local authorities at Piedras Negras. The two Mexicans, who had been employed by the United States as guides on army border crossings, were being held as traitors by the Mexican authorities. Shafter, in a flagrant violation of international law, planned to rescue the two guides by having the cavalry circle around Piedras Negras and come in from the rear while the infantry moved in from the front. The command moved to the field in early April with three companies of cavalry and two companies of infantry. One officer gave this eyewitness account:

> At early dawn as soon as we could see to move in-
> telligently, Schofield [major in the Tenth Cavalry]
> crossed with two companies of infantry. I accom-
> panied the latter command, we were challenged and
> threatened by a small party but no other opposition
> was made. The detachment landed and moving
> rapidly, occupied the main plaza, seizing the jail in
> which the prisoners were supposed to be confined.
> The door of the cell was found open as well as the
> entrance, and the jail deserted. Shortly afterwards
> the cavalry came in from the rear. The prisoners
> had I think been removed in the early part of the
> night. The Mexicans having learned that interest
> was taken by U.S. authorities in the men . . . had
> confederates on this side to give alarm. . . . While
> [the town was] held, no violence was done to any
> citizen, no shot fired—Everything was conducted in
> the most orderly and soldierly manner.[52]

After Shafter's expedition failed to secure the release of the
prisoners, General E. O. C. Ord, the commander of the
Department of Texas, sent word to the governor of Coahuila stating that if any harm should come to the two
Mexican guides, he would consider it an act of cooperation
with the raiders.[53] What eventually happened to the two
guides is left unclear, but it can be assumed that the Mexican authorities dealt with them as they saw fit.

Finally, increased raids and lack of cooperation from
the Mexican government led the United States to adopt a
more aggressive policy. In June 1877, President Rutherford
B. Hayes defined the United States position regarding the
border problems in instructions issued by the Secretary of
War.[54] The Mexican government, notified of the new policy, immediately issued a formal protest. Although Mexican
troops were instructed to cooperate with the Americans in
punishing the raiders, they were ordered to meet with force
any attempt by United States troops to cross the border.[55]

The black infantry was a part of almost every expedition that marched across the Rio Grande into Mexico. The constant use of the men of the Twenty-fourth and Twenty-fifth infantries in these expeditions would seem to indicate the confidence the frontier commanders had in these regiments. One white officer of the Twenty-fourth Infantry, Lieutenant John L. Bullis, became famous for his daring sorties into Mexico with his Seminole-Negro scouts, and their exploits are among the most interesting tales of the army on the Texas border.[56]

The black infantry regiments had one more important role to play before they were transferred from the Texas frontier. Men from these regiments were engaged in a series of skirmishes which prevented the famous Apache warrior Victorio from entering Texas. In August 1879 Victorio fled the Fort Stanton, New Mexico, reservation and began raiding settlements and attacking small army units in the field, leaving a trail of death and destruction behind him. For a year Victorio had eluded the army's attempts to capture him. When it would appear that the army was closing in on him, Victorio would cross into Mexico and take refuge in the mountains. In the spring of 1880 General Ord received orders from General Philip N. Sheridan to send the Tenth Cavalry to New Mexico to assist the Ninth Cavalry in capturing the elusive Victorio. Colonel Benjamin H. Grierson, commanding the Tenth Cavalry, was convinced that Victorio's next move would be a Texas raid and objected to moving his unit from Texas. Ord agreed with him and prevailed upon Sheridan to withdraw his order.[57]

In preparation for Victorio's anticipated move out of Mexico into Texas, Grierson made a change in tactics. Instead of following the usual procedure of chasing the Indians on long and often fruitless pursuits, he proposed to guard the waterholes and mountain passes which Victorio, his men, and horses must use to enter Texas. In July 1880 Grierson moved to the field with the Tenth Cavalry and units from the Twenty-fourth Infantry. At the same time, Colonel Valle of the Mexican Army was in the field with a command of 420 men in a joint effort to capture Victorio.

Shortly after Grierson moved to his base camp at Eagle Springs, Texas, he received word that the Mexican forces had met Victorio a few days before and fought an indecisive engagement. The battle had occurred near Ojo del Pino, Mexico, approximately fifty miles southwest of Eagle Springs. After the fight the Mexican force had withdrawn to a position opposite Fort Quitman, Texas. When word was received of the disposition of the Mexican command, Grierson went to Fort Quitman only to find Colonel Valle and his troops out of supplies and in desperate need of rations. He immediately authorized an issue of 1,000 pounds of flour and 1,130 pounds of grain to Colonel Valle for his hungry men. Because the Mexicans had left the field, Grierson was certain that Victorio's band would attempt to cross into Texas, and so he left Fort Quitman on July 29 for Eagle Springs to prepare his detachments for the probable crossing. For the next several days Grierson and his men played a deadly game of hide-and-seek with Victorio's Indians, managing to be one jump ahead of them by anticipating their moves to the various mountain passes and waterholes.[58]

On the afternoon of August 5, a supply train, guarded by Captain Gilmore and Company H of the Twenty-fourth Infantry, approached Grierson's position at Rattlesnake Springs. The supply train was rounding a mountain about eight miles northeast of the springs when it was attacked by the Indians. The raiders, seeing only a small force guarding the wagons, charged with great confidence and were astonished at the reception they received from the black infantrymen. The deadly rifle fire of Captain

Gilmore and his men forced the Indians to make a rapid retreat, costing them one dead and several wounded. The infantry suffered no casualties.[59]

For the next few days the black cavalry was out on continual scout and the black infantry was positioned at all the strategic waterholes. Captain Gilmore and his black infantrymen were ordered to accompany Colonel Grierson and two of his officers on an assignment that was best suited to the infantry. Grierson and Company H scaled the rough and precipitous cliffs of the Sierra Diablo, some 2,000 feet high, and scouted over the mountains as far as practicable, eliminating even the Sierra Diablo as a sanctuary for Victorio.[60]

It was a demoralized Victorio who was forced to retreat across the Rio Grande into Mexico on August 24, 1880. The Tenth Cavalry and the Twenty-fourth Infantry had successfully prevented him from using the vital waterholes and key mountain passes in his efforts to move into Texas. Victorio had been outmaneuvered and forced to retreat at the hands of an all-black command. The efforts of the black soldiers in their dogged pursuit of the elusive Victorio added an important and decisive chapter to the pacification of the Texas frontier. Victorio never again set foot on United States soil. On October 19, 1880, the Mexican Army surrounded and killed him and most of his warriors in the Tres Castillos Mountains of Mexico.[61]

In 1880 a decade of hard and honorable service came to an end for the Twenty-fourth and Twenty-fifth infantries. After ten years duty together the two regiments were to part company. Their Texas years were perhaps best summed up by Colonel Grierson on the occasion of dissolving the District of the Pecos on the Texas frontier.

> It is proper to refer to the services rendered by the officers and soldiers of the 10th Cavalry, and those of the 24th and 25th Infantry, who participated in

the arduous work and active field operations of the past three years.

In addition to the work at posts and sub-posts on barracks and quarters, and in guarding mails and other public property throughout the District; over one thousand miles of wagon roads and three hundred miles of telegraph lines have been constructed and kept in repair by the labor of troops, a vast region thoroughly scouted over, minutely explored, its resources made known and wonderfully developed.

The distance marched by companies and detachments during the three years specified, as shown by the records, foots up the grand total of one hundred and thirty-five thousand, seven hundred and ten (135,710) miles.

Much credit is due the troops who took part in the hard work, explorations, active scouting, expeditions against Mescalero Apaches, and especially to those engaged in the campaign against Victorio and his band of hostile Indians who were outmarched, outmaneuvered, repeatedly headed off, disconcerted, met face to face, squarely fought, severely punished, driven into Mexico, badly crippled and demoralized, where—no longer able to hold together as an organized force—they fell easy prey to the attack of the Mexican troops and Indian scouts from the Sierra Madre.

A settled feeling of security, heretofore unkown prevails throughout western Texas, causing a rapid and permanent increase of the population and wealth of the state, which is gratifying to citizens, and the military who have been instrumental in bringing about this very satisfactory condition of affairs.

The value of all this work to the great state of Texas, as cited herein, can hardly be overestimated. . . .

The gallantry displayed and meritorious services

rendered, justly merit some special and suitable recognition from the government.[62]

The Twenty-fourth and Twenty-fifth infantries left Texas as top regiments, full of pride in the job they had accomplished, but never did they receive "special or suitable recognition from the government."

NOTES

1. Lieutenant Colonel E. W. Hinks to Colonel Joseph A. Mower, April, 1869, Letters Received, Adjutant General's Office, No. H 271, Record Group 94, National Archives (hereafter cited as RG and NA). Dates are given as they are found on the documents; in some instances the day and the month are not given.

2. U.S., Congress, House Executive Documents, *Annual Report of the Secretary of War, 1869–1870*, 41st Cong., 2d sess., I, 98.

3. *Chronological List of Actions with Indians from January 1, 1866 to January 1888*, Office Memoranda, Adjutant General's Office, n.d., NA.

4. Elizabeth B. Custer, *Tenting On the Plains*, pp. 677–678.

5. Edward S. Wallace, "General Ranald Slidell Mackenzie, Indian Fighting Cavalryman," *Southwestern Historical Quarterly*, LVI (January 1953), 384.

6. Report of inspection of the Twenty-fifth Infantry at San Antonio, Texas, by Lieutenant Colonel James H. Carleton, June 20, 1870, Letters Received, Inspector General's office, File No. T 21, RG 159, NA.

7. See Chapter 5 for an account of the educational program conducted in the black infantry regiments.

8. U.S., Congress, House Executive Documents, *Annual*

Report of the Secretary of War, 1870–1871, 41st Cong., 3d Sess., I, 76.

9. See Chapter 6 for a full discussion of the attempts to replace the black regiments with white troops.

10. Colonel J. J. Reynolds to Adjutant General E. D. Townsend, April, 1870, Letters Received, Adjutant General's Office, File No. T 113, RG 94, NA.

11. Ibid.

12. *Annual Report of the Secretary of War, 1870–1871,* 41.

13. Ibid.

14. Walter C. Conway, ed., "Colonel Edmund Shriver's Inspector-General's Report on Military Posts in Texas, November, 1872–January, 1873," *Southwestern Historical Quarterly,* LXVII (April 1964), 579.

15. Colonel G. L. Andrews to Assistant Adjutant General, Department of Texas, October 4, 1875, Letters Sent, Fort Davis, Texas, RG 393, NA.

16. Ibid.

17. Lieutenant Colonel James H. Carleton to the Inspector General, March, 1871, Letters Received, Inspector General's Office, File No. T 8, RG 159, NA.

18. Captain N. H. Davis to the Inspector General, October, 1875, Letters Received, Inspector General's Office, File No. D 113, RG 159, NA.

19. Chaplain George G. Mullins to the Adjutant General's Office, October 1, 1875, Fort Davis, Texas, G. G. Mullins, Appointment, Commission and Personal Branch Records, RG 94, NA.

20. Lieutenant Colonel William R. Shafter to Assistant Adjutant General, Department of Texas, February 24, 1872, Letters Sent, Fort Davis, Texas, RG 393, NA.

21. Post Returns, Fort Duncan, Texas, May 31, 1870, RG 98, NA.

22. Colonel G. L. Andrews' endorsement on letter from Department of Texas, February 19, 1875, Letters Sent, Fort Davis, Texas, RG 393, NA.

23. Regimental Returns, Twenty-fifth Infantry Regiment, April 23, 1875, RG 94, NA.

24. Post Returns, Fort Davis, Texas, November, 1871, RG 98, NA; U.S., Congress, House Committee on Military Affairs, House Miscellaneous Documents, No. 64, *Testimony on the Texas Border Troubles*, 45th Cong., 2d Sess., VI, (1877), 138.

25. Copy of Special Order Number 102, Department of Texas, San Antonio, Texas, May 31, 1872, William Rufus Shafter Papers, Stanford University Library.

26. Post Returns, Fort Duncan, Texas, February, 1880, RG 98, NA.

27. *Annual Report of the Secretary of War, 1870–1871*, 41.

28. Post Returns, Fort Davis, Texas, November, 1877, December, 1878, RG 98, NA.

29. Waterman L. Ormsby, *The Butterfield Overland Mail*, pp. 44–45, 48, 56, 63, 74, 77.

30. Sergeant B. Stow to Post Adjutant, Fort Stockton, Texas, October 2, 1873, Letters Received, Adjutant General's Office, File No. 4369, RG 94, NA.

31. Lieutenant Colonel William R. Shafter to F. C. Taylor, Fort Concho, Texas, January, 1872, Letters Sent, Fort Davis, Texas, RG 393, NA.

32. Lieutenant W. W. Landon to "Sergeant," Twenty-fifth Infantry, El Muerto, Texas, November 6, 1878, Letters Sent, Fort Davis, Texas, RG 393, NA.

33. Ormsby, *The Butterfield Mail*, pp. 164–166; J. W. Williams, "The Butterfield Overland Mail Road Across Texas," *Southwestern Historical Quarterly*, LXI (July 1957), 1–19; Kathryn S. McMillen, "A Descriptive Bibliography on the San Antonio-San Diego Mail Line," *Southwestern Historical Quarterly*, LIX (October 1955), 206–214.

34. Ormsby, *The Butterfield Mail*, pp. 14–15.

35. Regimental Returns, Twenty-fifth Infantry Regiment, October, 1877, RG 94, NA.

36. Colonel G. L. Andrews to Assistant Adjutant General, Department of Texas, July 21, 1877, Letters Sent, Fort Davis, Texas, RG 393, NA.

37. Ibid.

38. Upon referring to my Morning Report, I find that from August 2, 1874, to March 24, 1875, . . . my men have had as a

rule but "one night in bed," that during February, March and April, 1875 the greater part of the fatigue duty at the Post was performed by the Band; that during March 1875 two of my Infantry companies marched nearly 250 miles and in May and June another company marched 750 miles, in October, another company marched 225 miles; that during the year detachments have several times marched to Fort Quitman and Bliss, also to Fort Concho and once to San Antonio and returning, that during May and June last, the detachments from the Post will average one sixth of the garrison; . . . that more than once for ten successive days, being unable to fill the guard detail of but 12 privates until Retreat, have been obliged to take men who had been on stage escort the night previous, and the Post Commander's orderly; that even with my limited amount of transportation, teams have stood idle for several days at a time for want of men to drive them. . . .

Since September 1, 1875, one company of Cavalry and one of Infantry aggregating 73 men have made a scout, marching an aggregate of 1,153 miles and mapped the country.

In the foregoing I have simply enumerated such labors of my command as occurred most readily to my mind and are known of all men, feeling confident they alone effectually dispose of the accusation of "Idleness." Colonel G. L. Andrews to Assistant Adjutant General, Department of Texas, November, 1875, Letters Sent, Fort Davis, Texas, RG 393, NA.

39. U.S., Congress, House Executive Documents, *Annual Report of the Secretary of War, 1872–1873*, 42d Cong., 3d Sess., I, 55.

40. Regimental Returns, Twenty-fifth Infantry Regiment, January, 1872, RG 94, NA.

41. Lieutenant Colonel J. W. Davidson to Assistant Adjutant General, Department of Texas, August 27, 1874, Letters Received, Department of Texas, File No. 3490, RG 94, NA; William H. Leckie, *The Buffalo Soldiers,* pp. 120–123.

42. Lieutenant Colonel J. W. Davidson to Assistant Adjutant General. Department of Texas, August 27, 1874, Letters Received, Department of Texas, File No. 3490, RG 94, NA.

43. U.S., Congress, House Executive Documents, *Annual*

Report of the Secretary of War, 1874–1875, 43d Cong., 2d Sess., I, 42.

44. Headquarters, Department of Texas, to Lieutenant Colonel William R. Shafter, May 31, 1875, William Rufus Shafter Papers, Stanford University Library.

45. Leckie, *The Buffalo Soldiers*, pp. 147–148.

46. *Annual Report of the Secretary of War, 1874–1875*, p. 43–44.

47. J. Fred Rippy, "Some Precedents of the Pershing Expedition into Mexico," *Southwestern Historical Quarterly*, XXIV (April 1921), 300–301.

48. *Annual Report of the Secretary of War, 1874–1875*, p. 88.

49. U.S., Congress, House, Committee on Military Affairs, House Miscellaneous Documents, Document No. 64, *Testimony on the Texas Border Troubles*, 45th Cong., 2d Sess., 1877, VI, 7.

50. Post Returns, Fort Clark, Texas, May, 1873, RG 98, NA.

51. Leckie, *The Buffalo Soldiers*, p. 228.

52. Report of the Assistant Adjutant General J. H. Taylor to General E. O. C. Ord, Department of Texas, April 5, 1877, William Rufus Shafter Papers, Stanford University Library.

53. U.S., Congress, House Executive Documents, No. 13, *Mexican Border Troubles*, 45th Cong., 1st Sess., 1877, p. 12.

54. The President desires that the utmost vigilance on the part of the military forces in Texas be exercised for the suppression of these raids. It is very desirable that efforts to this end, in so far at least as they necessarily involve operations on both sides of the border, be made with the cooperation of the Mexican authorities, and to inform them that while the President is anxious to avoid giving offense to Mexico, he is nevertheless convinced that the invasion of our territory by armed and organized bodies of thieves and robbers to prey upon our citizens should not be longer endured.

General Ord will at once notify the Mexican authorities along the Texas border, of the great desire of the President to unite with them in efforts to suppress this long continued lawlessness. At the same time he will inform those authorities that if the Government of Mexico shall continue to neglect the duty of suppressing these outrages, that duty will devolve upon this government, and will be performed, even if its performance should render necessary the occasional crossing of the border by our troops. You will, therefore, direct General Ord that in case the lawless incursions continue he will be at liberty, in the use of his own discretion when in pursuit of a band of the marauders, and when his troops are either in sight of them or upon a fresh trail, to follow them across the Rio Grande, and to overtake and punish them, as well as retake stolen property taken from our citizens and found in their hands on the Mexican side of the line." Ibid., pp. 14–15.

55. Ibid., pp. 20–21.

56. Edward S. Wallace, "General John Lapham Bullis, Thunderbolt of the Texas Frontier, I," *Southwestern Historical Quarterly*, LIV (April 1951), 452–461; Edward S. Wallace, "General John Lapham Bullis, Thunderbolt of the Texas Frontier, II," *Southwestern Historical Quarterly*, LV (July 1951), 77–85; Kenneth W. Porter, "The Seminole-Negro Scouts, 1870–1881," *Southwestern Historical Quarterly*, LV (January 1952), 358–377. These articles provide an account of the exploits of Bullis and his scouts while serving on the Texas frontier. This group was called Seminole-Negro scouts because their ancestors were for the most part runaway slaves who had taken refuge among the Seminole Indians in Florida. They were generally assigned to one of the four black regiments.

57. U.S., Congress, House Executive Documents, *Annual Report of the Secretary of War, 1880–1881*, 46th Cong., 3d Sess., II, 159; Leckie, *The Buffalo Soldiers*, pp. 222–223.

58. *Annual Report of the Secretary of War, 1880–1881*, pp. 159–160.

59. Ibid., p. 161.

60. Ibid., p. 163.

61. Leckie, *The Buffalo Soldiers*, p. 228.

62. Twenty-fifth Infantry Regiment Scrapbook, United States Army Command Mobile, RG 391, NA. This scrapbook was compiled by Captain John H. Nankivell and all items and

documents are marked as certified true copies of the originals. Many of the orders are included as they were printed. Most of the material in this scrapbook was used in the writing of Nankivell's book, *History of the Twenty-fifth Regiment, United States Infantry, 1869–1926.*

3

The Twenty-Fifth
Infantry in the Dakotas
and Montana

The army's decision to move the Twenty-fourth and
Twenty-fifth Infantries from Texas was made only after
substantial debate over where to send them. There had
been considerable pressure from the officers of the regiments to have their units moved closer to civilization. Some
officers, particularly those in the Twenty-fourth, had been
on frontier duty since 1867. Such service was a hardship
on the families of officers and men, since housing, schools,
stores, and other conveniences identified with established
communities were sorely inadequate.[1] Some officers, unwilling to subject their families to these privations, had re-
signed their commissions rather than remain at frontier
posts. Many enlisted men, discouraged by the isolation of the
western forts, refused to re-enlist because of the oppres-
siveness of their assignment. The army was not indifferent
to the problems these regiments faced and the kind of
service they were required to perform. General E. O. C.
Ord, the commanding general of the Department of Texas,
in his annual report of 1878 stated his views in this way:

> I would like to impress upon the government, that
> the officers and men who stay and scout with their
> commands, out in the desert districts of Texas, and
> perform their full duties, are entitled to something
> more than commendation.
>
> The climate of these deserts is, for the most
> part, rigorous, and the troops are subject to ex-
> tremes of heat in summer and cold in winter, with
> frequent privations, such as hunger and thirst. It
> would not be regarded by them as a hardship, and
> would redound to the advantage of all concerned, if
> the regiments that have, for so many years endured
> such service, could take their turn for duty in the
> vicinity of civilization. I refer especially to the
> Tenth Infantry and the colored troops.[2]

In the early months of 1879, discussions were initiated
at the War Department concerning the feasibility of moving the Twenty-fourth and Twenty-fifth infantries off the
Mexican border. The Adjutant General wrote to General
C. C. Auger, former commander of the Department of
Texas, who was at that time commanding the Department
of the South, to obtain his opinion on where to move the
black regiments. It had been suggested that the Twenty-
fourth be stationed at New Orleans and at Little Rock,
Arkansas, but General Augur thought it unwise to send
the black regiment to either city, fearing that the presence
of black troops in the South would cause trouble. He
stated, "However senseless and unreasonable it may be regarded, there is no doubt of the fact that a strong prejudice exists at [*sic*] the South against colored troops."[3]
Augur also expressed concern that if the Twenty-fourth
was stationed in a locality where a large proportion of
the inhabitants were black it would seriously increase the
possibility of racial troubles. He implied that if any trouble
were to occur between the white and black communities,

the black soldiers would become involved because of their strong feelings for the rights of Negroes.[4]

General Augur's letter was forwarded through army channels with opinions added at each level of command. General Winfield S. Hancock, the commanding general of the Military Division of the Atlantic, concurred with General Augur's recommendations and commented that it would be no great improvement for the officers and men of the Twenty-fourth Infantry to move from Texas to Louisiana. General William T. Sherman was in favor of the change, saying: "The Tenth Infantry, a white regiment, is to be changed next month for the reason that it has been 10 years on the Rio Grande. Shall one rule apply to a white regiment, and another to a black?"[5] Secretary of War G. W. McCrary's remarks contained President Rutherford B. Hayes' view that black troops should be kept on duty in the South with some provision to relieve the officers for part-time service in the North or West.[6] Apparently, President Hayes' primary concern was for the welfare of the white officers and not the black enlisted men.

In the course of the discussions it was suggested that the black regiments be sent to the Department of Dakota. There was at that time, however, a common belief that black people could not exist in cold climates. This stemmed from the notion that since blacks came originally from the hot and humid jungles of Africa and had lived in the warm climate of the South, they would be unable to adapt to cold weather. It was this concept that prompted the Quartermaster General to oppose a transfer of the regiments to the North. He stated that orders sending black troops to Dakota Territory would mean death and sickness to the men of the regiment. "Colored men will not enlist with the prospects of going to that rigorous climate . . . the effect of the cold will be very injurious to those men whose terms of enlistment do not soon expire."[7] When orders were issued in April 1880 to send the Twenty-fifth Infantry to the Department of Dakota, many officers were certain the change in climate would prove a serious hardship for the black soldiers. Others saw it only as an experiment. To the officers and men of the Twenty-fifth it was a welcome change of scenery and duty.

The Twenty-fifth notified all its units in May 1880 of the transfer orders and arranged for their transportation out of Texas. The headquarters unit, the band, and three companies assembled at Fort Concho on June 3 and marched 246 miles to the railroad station at San Antonio.[8] For the next eight weeks the companies of the Twenty-fifth departed Texas at irregular intervals by train with the last company arriving in Dakota Territory on August 17. When the regiment was finally settled in, it was garrisoned at three posts in the Department of Dakota: Fort Hale, Fort Meade, and, as headquarters, Fort Randall.[9]

Although the quarters at Fort Randall were considerably better than at Fort Davis, Texas, they still did not provide easy living. In 1881 an inspector noted that the barracks were overcrowded, in need of repairs, lacking proper lighting, and short of furniture.[10] Reports from Fort Hale indicated that the companies there were living under worse conditions than at Fort Randall. Captain R. P. Hughes of the Third Infantry made an inspection of Fort Hale in 1883 and was appalled at the condition of the barracks. He reported, "The post commander has his post in excellent condition as to cleanliness and order, but he cannot make a tumble down log hut look either beautiful or inviting."[11] Hughes also stated that both the officers' quarters and the enlisted men's barracks were made of cottonwood logs and in all cases the bottom logs were decayed and the corners were falling down. It seemed to him that the whole fort was coming down in ruins.

> I respectfully submit to the Department Commander
> that these two companies are so much more badly
> off than any of the other troops in this geographical
> department that I think some strong measures
> should be adopted for their relief. . . . The troops
> are good, but their accommodations are wretched.[12]

For the companies at Fort Hale the move to Dakota Territory had meant little change except in scenery and climate.

The units stationed at Fort Meade were the most fortunate of the regiment as far as living quarters were concerned. They shared the post with six companies of the
Seventh Cavalry whose barracks and officers' quarters were
ample, comfortable, and maintained in good condition.[13] An
inspection report in 1881 stated that not only was the garrison in excellent condition but the kitchen and mess facilities
were outstanding.[14] Fort Meade continued to be improved,
and in 1887 Colonel J. G. Tilford of the Seventh Cavalry,
commander of the post, declared, "I believe that on the
whole this post will compare favorably with any other of
its size and advantages in the army."[15]

In addition to the change in scenery and climate the
Twenty-fifth found that the nature of its duties differed
also. In Dakota Territory there were no station guards or
stagecoach escorts nor were there regular scouting patrols
to make. A few work assignments, such as telegraph construction and repair, were still on the duty roster, and the
colder climate added a new task: wood cutting details to
supply fuel for heat and cooking at the northern forts.[16]
These crews would be out for weeks at a time clearing out
timber and hauling it back to the post. Generally, when a
company was responsible for bringing in the wood, it
would take all of its available men into the field, using
wagons to haul the timber back to garrison or rafting the
logs downriver.[17] Either way, woodcutting was hard work
and not a favored chore by anyone.

Protecting railroad tie-cutting crews was another obligation in Dakota that kept the men in the field for long periods of time. The railroad crews worked in isolated areas, and the army was responsibile for defending them against possible Indian attacks. A detail consisting of two companies of the Seventh Cavalry and a company of the Twenty-fifth Infantry left Fort Meade on May 2, 1881, for the purpose of safeguarding the Northern Pacific Railroad tie-cutting crews. The small command, under Captain F. W. Benteen of the Seventh Cavalry, went 135 miles to Camp Cook in Montana Territory, where they remained guarding the railroad crews until June 29 when they were relieved by other troops from the Seventh Cavalry and the Twenty-fifth. The latter detachment remained in the field with the tie-cutting operation until October 25.[18]

Because most of the Indians in the Dakota area stayed on their reservations, depredations were not as common as they were in Texas. Still, there was occasional concern over the possibility of Indian trouble. In the summer of 1882 two companies of the Twenty-fifth left Fort Randall with orders to protect the settlers on the Keya Paha and Montana Rivers who were alarmed because Sun Dances were being held at the Rosebud Indian Agency. The most important religious ritual of the Plains Indians, the Sun Dance brought together several tribes during the summer months to observe this eight-day rite. The dances generated a religious fervor which might lead the tribes to become warlike or commit depredations.[19] The two infantry companies arrived near the reservation on June 30 and maintained constant surveilance along the roads and rivers in the vicinity of Keya. A month later, after the Indian scare had subsided, they returned to Fort Randall. During their time in the field the two companies had marched over 300 miles on patrol.[20] Although no outbreaks of violence occurred, the presence of the black infantry provided a great measure of security for the settlers.

The spring of 1881 found the officers and men of the Twenty-fifth providing disaster relief for many settlers in Dakota Territory. After an extremely severe winter in which the snow never disappeared from the ground, there were floods throughout the territory. Many settlers' homes were swept away along with all their belongings. Crops were ruined and livestock drowned in the high water. During the months of April and May, Captain H. B. Quimby with Company F of the Twenty-fifth, made several trips to the settlements along the Keya Paha River to relieve the hungry and homeless settlers in that area. Approximately 800 men, women, and children were assisted by Company F. The expense of this relief was borne by the government and by donations from the men of the Twenty-fifth. One incident at Fort Randall symbolizes the concern shown by the men of the Twenty-fifth for the plight of the settlers. A herd of cattle belonging to a nearby farmer was pastured near the river and was in danger of being swept away by the rising water until the black soldiers drove the livestock to safety on the military reservation.[21]

The fall of 1881 found the Twenty-fifth Infantry in the company of one of the most famous of all Plains Indians. After the Battle of the Little Big Horn, the Sioux Indians, still flush with victory and a little careless, were caught in an army trap on October 31, 1876 and forced to surrender. Except for a few rebellious bands that continued to roam the hills, most of the Indians had moved onto reservations. Within a few years most of the recalcitrant bands had drifted back to the reservations and prepared to accept their fate at the hands of the white man. Sitting Bull and a band of his warriors refused to submit and fled into Canada where they remained until the threat of starvation eventually forced them to surrender to the United States Army.[22] On Saturday evening, September 17, 1881, Captain H. S. Howe of the Seventeenth Infantry arrived at Fort Randall on board the steamer *General Sher-*

Captain Charles Bentzoni, Twenty-fifth Infantry, with his wife and child visiting Sitting Bull and his family at Fort Randall, Dakota Territory, 1882.

The Regimental Band and a Battalion of the Twenty-fifth Infantry at Fort Randall, Dakota Territory, 1882.

Company I of the 25th Infantry Regiment at Fort Snelling, Minnesota in the 1880s.

Captain Charles Bentzoni and Company B of the Twenty-fifth Infantry at Fort Randall, Dakota Territory, 1882.

man with Sitting Bull and 166 of his people in custody. They were sent from Fort Yates to Fort Randall to be held as prisoners of war.[23]

During Sitting Bull's internment at Fort Randall there was never a serious problem or disturbance. A mutual respect developed between the old warrior and the officers and men of the Twenty-fifth. A popular historian has written of Sitting Bull's stay at the fort:

> Sitting Bull was agreeably surprised by his treatment as a prisoner of war. Though many of the soldiers and officers there must have regarded him as the man who killed Custer, they showed the old warrior no discourtesy. Though monotonous, the life at Fort Randall was by no means disagreeable. The commanding officer and his subordinates exhibited the qualities and character traditional among officers of the best outfits of the Regular Army of the United States. Sitting Bull and his band had nothing to complain of on that score.[24]

It was a fine compliment for the Twenty-fifth Infantry even though the author neglected to mention that the "outfit" at Fort Randall was a black regiment.

In 1881 Sitting Bull asked that Colonel George L. Andrews, the commanding officer of the Twenty-fifth, write a letter requesting permission for him and a group of warriors to go to Washington to parley with the United States government in order to be informed as to the government's plans for him and his people. Colonel Andrews wrote the letter adding his opinion that Sitting Bull and his people would submit without trouble to almost anything reasonable, but that some kind of action should be taken promptly.[25] As it turned out, Sitting Bull did not go to Washington nor did the President act with speed to tell him his plans. In fact, he remained at Fort Randall until

May, 1883, when he and his band were put aboard a steamer bound for Standing Rock Agency located near Fort Yates, Dakota Territory.[26]

While most of the men were busy discharging the necessary fatigue guard duties, one unit of the regiment was actively engaged in projecting a favorable public image of black soldiers. Since the early days in Texas, the regimental band had been the pride and joy of the Twenty-fifth Infantry. Its concerts were the source of many hours of pleasure to the officers and men and offered a welcome relief from the monotony of the isolated Texas posts. Through the years the regiment was able to enlist bandmasters with the ability to train musicians, so that by the time the Twenty-fifth was transferred to the Department of Dakota it had many skilled and experienced musicians. Their musical repertoire and a flair for showmanship made the black musicians popular wherever they performed. It was not long before they were requested to appear at various public functions throughout Dakota Territory. On September 13, 1883, the band, joined by a company of infantry, left Fort Snelling in Minnesota for Rochester where they were invited to play for the crowds at the Minnesota State Fair.[27] Earlier in the summer the band had provided the music at the commencement exercises of the Shattuck Military School near Minneapolis. The commandant of the school wrote to Lieutenant Colonel M. M. Blunt of the Twenty-fifth, expressing his appreciation for the unit's performance. His letter indicated that the regiment's musical reputation was well known: "The Band proved to be all that we had expected from the reports which had reached us before we heard them, skilled in the use of their instruments and orderly in their deportment."[28] During its tour in Dakota Territory, the popularity of the Twenty-fifth Infantry musicians continued to grow and they were in constant demand for public concerts.[29] Apparently, many citizens in the territory were favorably disposed toward the Twenty-fifth because of its fine regimental band.

Still, there were those living near the posts where the Twenty-fifth was stationed, who were apprehensive about the presence of black soldiers. They no doubt recalled the outbreaks of violence that had occurred between black troops and the white populace in the South during Reconstruction. Sentiment favoring the removal of the black troops from Dakota surfaced following a murder and lynching in Sturgis City, Dakota Territory, adjacent to Fort Meade.

A doctor in Sturgis City named, ironically, Lynch, was shot while reading in his office on the evening of August 22, 1885, supposedly out of jealousy over a woman. Corporal Hallon, a black soldier stationed at Fort Meade, was arrested the following day by civilian authorities on the basis of circumstantial evidence. On the night of August 25, a mob broke into the Sturgis City jail and lynched Hallon. Understandably, there was a great deal of anger on the part of the black troops at Fort Meade.

The excitement accompanying the lynching had hardly subsided when another murder occurred involving a squad of black infantrymen from Fort Meade. With the precision of a military firing squad, the black soldiers marched into Sturgis City late at night and proceeded single file down the main street, coming to a halt in front of a brothel-saloon owned by a man named Abe Hill. The leader of the squad stepped forward and shouted a warning for all soldiers to clear out of Hill's place. The squad then raised their rifles, fired several volleys into the saloon, did an about face, and marched down the street to a Mr. Dolan's house. Again they fired a volley into the building. After returning to Abe Hill's to fire a few more volleys into the saloon, the soldiers, marching in perfect cadence, retreated down the street and out of sight. A white man by the name of Robert S. Bell was killed in Abe Hill's place. Although the facts are not complete, the motive for the shooting appears to have been ill feeling between Hill, Dolan, and several black soldiers. Upon hearing the rifle fire in Sturgis City, the officers at Fort Meade immediately formed a detail to arrest all men absent from the post. Four infantrymen were arrested returning to the fort and charged with the shooting of Robert S. Bell.[30]

These disturbances led to a letter being sent to President Grover Cleveland by one B. G. Caulfield requesting the removal of the black troops from Fort Meade. Caulfield said that he was convinced the Twenty-fifth Infantry Regiment was composed, at least in part, of reckless desperadoes and that the citizens of the area would benefit by their transfer to another post.[31] The letter was referred to General A. H. Terry, the commander of the Department of Dakota. Terry's attitude toward the black soldiers was both fair and reasonable. He recommended the black troops not be removed from their present post, since the actions of a few did not prove that the men at Fort Meade were desperadoes. The general praised the black soldiers and cited the fact that they were less troublesome than white soldiers. He also said that he was sure the officers at the post would take the necessary steps to prevent a similar occurrence in the future. His closing remarks revealed what he considered to be the real source of the problems between Sturgis City and the black troops at Fort Meade. Terry suggested that the citizens of Sturgis City, in permitting brothels to do business, were as much to blame as the black soldiers for any difficulties. "Had no such place existed it is most improbable that any affray would have occurred, and if the people of Sturgis City suffer such places to exist, they must, I submit, expect the natural result of their existence. . . ."[32] It was to General Terry's credit that he saw through the racial overtones that permeated the issue and spoke to the basic problem. His recommendation that the troops remain was accepted by President Cleveland.

During its Dakota years the Twenty-fifth continued to prove itself a competent army organization. According to the inspection reports of those years, the black infantry was an effective and efficient army regiment. In relation to the army's biggest personnel problem, desertion, the Twenty-fifth and its sister regiment the Twenty-fourth could claim the lowest desertion rate in the army. It was the Dakota years that enabled the regiment to destroy the old myth that black troops could not serve in cold northern climates.

Early in the spring of 1888 the Twenty-fifth Infantry received orders to exchange stations with the Third Infantry garrisoned in the Montana Territory. The black regiment left its Dakota posts late in May 1888 and traveled to its new forts in Montana. The headquarters, the band, and four companies were garrisoned at Fort Missoula while four more companies moved in at Fort Shaw and the other two companies called Fort Custer home. For most of the units of the regiment the transfer meant better living quarters than those they had left in Dakota. The barracks at Fort Missoula, for example, were in relatively good condition and in need of only minor repairs.[33]

For eighteen years the Twenty-fifth Infantry band, the pride of the regiment, had not been properly quartered, and the move to Fort Missoula proved no exception. Colonel Andrews wrote to the headquarters of the Department of Dakota stating that the band was temporarily living in a crude, oversize log cabin and requested appropriations for the construction of adequate housing for the musicians. Conditions were so bad that during the winter months the men had to board up one portion of the building and patch the cracks between the logs to enable them to heat it to a comfortable temperature.[34] Living accommodations for officers also continued to be a problem. When orders were received at Fort Missoula assigning Chaplain George W. Simpson to the post, Colonel Andrews advised against sending him to the regiment. One reason he gave was that the post was near enough to Missoula to allow the officers and men to attend religious services in town. But, he also stated, his primary consideration was the critical shortage of housing for officers.[35] It was not uncommon for frontier army posts in the West to have two and sometimes three families living in one set of officer's quarters.

The black infantry companies had been in garrison at Fort Shaw only a few weeks when they were stunned by the lynching of one of their men at Sun River, Montana Territory. Jealousy over a woman began a chain of events that led to the lynching of Private Robert Robinson at the hands of a group of masked men. Robinson was keeping a mistress named Queeny Montgomery who had followed him from Fort Sisseton, Dakota Territory, to Fort Shaw. He had moved Queeny into a shack on the edge of Sun River. A Private Matchett of the Third Infantry had remained behind at Fort Shaw to finish out the last few days of his enlistment and was apparently sharing Queeny's affections. One evening in June 1888, Private Robinson went to Queeny's house and found Matchett with her. In a jealous rage, Robinson took his rifle and beat Matchett, breaking his arm and jaw. Matchett was able to escape from the house and fled into the darkness with Robinson in hot pursuit.

Hearing the commotion, a crowd gathered in front of the Maud S Stables; Robinson, running down the street, stopped and asked the assembled group if they had seen a white soldier. The reply was that they had not. One member of the crowd, Charles Maguire by name, clapped his hands as Robinson was turning to leave and said, "Let's go and see what is the fun."[36] At this Robinson raised his rifle, which had gone unnoticed in the darkness, and shot Maguire through the head. Immediately, several bystanders attempted to apprehend Robinson but he eluded them and returned to Fort Shaw.

When news of the shooting reached Fort Shaw, Robinson was arrested and placed under guard. The following day, Sheriff Downing of Sun River and his deputy went to Fort Shaw and the commanding officer turned Robinson over to them. The sheriff took his prisoner to Sun River and put him in jail, a decision that later proved to be a serious mistake. Although there had been talk of a lynching, the town appeared quiet to Sheriff Downing when he returned with his prisoner. At midnight on June 10, 1888, two masked men, followed by several others wearing masks, walked quietly into the jail and demanded the key from the surprised deputy. Robinson was removed from the jail, taken to the alley behind Stone's Store, and lynched; his body was left dangling over the alleyway.[37]

When news of the shooting and rumors of a possible lynching reached Great Falls, some twenty miles away, Judge Thomas Bach, the presiding judge of the area, immediately dispatched two deputies to ride as fast as they could to Sun River to assist Sheriff Downing in case of trouble. The two lawmen reached Sun River in time to assist the sheriff and his deputy in the search for Robinson, whose body was not discovered until about daybreak. A short time later, Judge Bach, accompanied by another deputy, drove into Sun River in a buckboard. Although the judge was disgusted by the lynching and made his feelings known to the community, those responsible for the outrage were never brought to justice.[38]

In spite of this unpleasant beginning, the Twenty-fifth Infantry found a relatively favorable climate of opinion for their regiment in Montana. As had been the case in the Dakota Territory, the regimental band proved extremely popular with the local citizenry. The first public appearance of the band at Missoula, in the Memorial Day parade of 1888, drew high praise from the local newspaper.

> About 2:30 p.m. the procession formed on Higgins Avenue, headed by the band of the Twenty-fifth U.S. Infantry, which came over from the Fort to assist in the observance of the day, and which discoursed the sweetest music ever heard in Missoula along the line of march.[39]

Not only was the black infantry band a part of nearly all civic and patriotic celebrations, it also presented regular concerts in Missoula every Thursday evening. An incident at one of these evening concerts provided the local newspaper editor with an opportunity to compliment the army musicians and vent his disgust at some noisy traveling medicine men.

> The weekly concert given Thursday evening by the 25th U.S. Infantry band, was the finest they have yet given. The selections were new to most of our people and were rendered with a degree of proficiency hard to excel. The only feature that tended as a drawback toward the evening's entertainment, was the appearance of a couple of patent medicine quacks with patent leather cheek and a gall as hard and as large as a grindstone whose aim was to drown the music of the band with one loud, discordant yell.[40]

The reputation of the band was soon known throughout most of Montana and the regimental commander, Colonel George L. Andrews, received numerous requests for its appearance from different parts of the territory. In reply he was cautious to state, "I presume you are aware that the 25th Infantry band, is composed of colored men."[41] The talented black musicians were largely responsible for the friendly relations that existed between the people of Missoula and the Twenty-fifth. An indication of the extent to which the musical organization was accepted by the community is found in a newspaper obituary notice. Captain C. P. Higgins, one of Missoula's most prominent citizens died in October 1889, and his funeral was attended by dignitaries from various parts of the Northwest. Conspicuous among the many groups in the funeral procession was the Twenty-fifth Infantry band. As a matter of fact, they even marched in front of the Masons.[42]

The regiment's tour of duty in Montana Territory found it performing the same basic assignments that it had in Dakota. The one major difference was that by 1888 its duty stations were not isolated posts in the wilderness. The railroads had connected Montana with the East, and the settlers were coming into the territory in greater numbers. Communities such as Missoula and Great Falls were towns with an established economic and social base. The threat of an Indian uprising had diminished to such a degree that only those settlements located on the boundaries of Indian reservations were apt to become alarmed.

One scare resulted from Indian unrest on the Flathead Indian Reservation at Ravalli, Montana Territory. On June 11, 1889, the local sheriff had asked for army assistance in arresting some Indians suspected of murder. After discussing the matter with Colonel George L. Andrews, the sheriff decided not to attempt to make the arrests. Then on the afternoon of June 24, 1889 a deputy sheriff arrived at Fort Missoula excitedly asking for both troops and weapons for use at the Flathead Reservation. To both requests Colonel Andrews gave a negative reply, stating that he could act only upon petition of the Indian Agent. The next day shortly after noon, a telegram was received from agent Peter Ronan asking that troops be dispatched immediately to the reservation to prevent the outbreak of trouble. Andrews learned that the sheriff had decided on his own to attempt to arrest the suspected murderers and that an Indian had been shot, causing a great deal of unrest on the reservation. The same afternoon, three companies under the command of Captain Gaines Lawson arrived at the reservation where agent Ronan met them at the railroad station and suggested that they camp there until the results of an Indian council were known. As it turned out no outbreak occurred, mainly because the presence of the black soldiers allowed cooler heads to prevail among the Indians. Most of Lawson's troops left the reservation on July 9, although one company was left behind until July 12 at the request of the governor of Montana.[43]

The Twenty-fifth was called out again in April 1890, this time in response to pleas from settlers north of Flathead Lake in northwestern Montana. They sought army protection from attacks by vagabond reservation Indians and members of Canadian tribes. A company of the regiment with Captain D. B. Wilson in command was dispatched from Fort Missoula on April 7, 1890. He was ordered to report on the state of affairs, and particularly on the attitude of the Indians living in the region. After investigating the situation, Wilson sent word to Colonel Andrews that there appeared little probability of serious trouble. It was his opinion that if the civil authorities prohibited the sale of liquor to Indians and half-breeds it would solve most of the Indian problems. The company remained at their base in Demersville, Montana, for two months, with small detachments out scouting for renegade Indians. In July it was relieved by another black infantry company which remained in the area until ordered back to Fort Missoula in September 1890.[44]

Practice marches and maneuvers, required by army regulations at least once a year, also took the men of the Twenty-fifth out in the field.[45] These exercises, which kept the companies occupied for about two weeks and were usually conducted in September or October, conditioned the men as professional soldiers and provided the officers an opportunity to instruct the troops in various types of field problems. The infantrymen were taught how to manufacture gabions and fascines, as well as the proper method of digging rifle pits. Military movements and tactics were also included in the field training on each practice march.[46]

Besides the regular field duty, occasionally a company would be detailed to carry out some special project. In October 1889 Company A left Fort Custer for detached service at the Custer battlefield. It had been asked to place 106 headstones at the military cemetery to mark the graves of officers, men, and civilians whose remains had been moved from the site of old Fort Phil Kearney, Wyoming.[47] In the spring of 1890 another company of the Twenty-fifth from Fort Custer spent two weeks marking the boundaries of the cemetery at the Custer battlefield and erecting new headstones.[48] Public service assignments such as these were appreciated by the men as a welcome change from the routine of garrison life.

With regular duty hours and more leisure time on post, the officers of the Twenty-fifth Infantry were faced with having to provide adequate recreation for the men. In the early part of 1889, it was suggested that forts should examine the possibility of eliminating the civilian post traders and operating their own canteens. The advocates of this plan argued that the canteen could be managed by the officers and staffed with dependable enlisted men, with the profits being earmarked for the post school, the post library, garden supplies, and additional food for the mess halls. Gambling and hard liquor would be prohibited at these post-operated canteens.

Colonel Andrews spoke out in favor of retaining the post trader, reasoning that the post trader who ran a billiards room and a bar located just off post furnished a more practical outlet for the recreational needs of the men. It was more conducive to good discipline, declared Andrews, to maintain the trader's clubroom because it kept many of the men near the fort who otherwise would be getting into trouble in town. He added that he knew of only a few officers who would be willing to become the manager of a coffee house, a billiards room, or a beer garden.[49]

The post trader's clubroom at Fort Missoula, although popular with the men of the Twenty-fifth because it provided a convenient place to loaf, talk, and drink, was not entirely effective in keeping the more adventurous soldier from going into town and getting into trouble. From time immemorial the soldiers' temptations were women and whiskey, and the men of the black infantry were no exception. The local newspapers carried accounts of various incidents involving men of the Twenty-fifth, women, or whiskey or both. One story dealing with the troubles of a soldier and whiskey appeared in the *Weekly Missoulian* in November 1889.

COLORED SAM GRISWOLD DONATES $40
TO THE COUNTY COURT

Yesterday afternoon, the negro who was arrested for the indiscriminate use of a six-shooter on Sunday, was up before Judge Sloan to explain his actions. The principal witnesses were the driver of Hawke's hack and a fiery haired mongrel claiming the poetic name of Virgie Lee.

Sam Griswold, the colored soldier, admitted he was pretty drunk on Sunday afternoon and did not know much about what he did. The testimony only showed that Griswold used his revolver just to have a little fun. For this fun Judge Sloan charged him $40 and costs of trial. Owing to a scarcity of the wherewithal to settle accounts, Griswold was placed in the county jail, but he has hopes of being able to pay his fine today as yesterday was pay day at the post.[50]

The editor's style suggests an attitude current among some whites at the time: that black people were clownish and amusing to watch. A month later another account written in the same manner, and detailing the difficulties of a soldier with both whiskey and women appeared in the same paper.

> Yesterday one of the colored soldiers at Fort Missoula named Jacob Jones was brought before Justice Logan charged with making an assault on Lizzie Maroney of the notorious "Four-mile" house. It seems that Jones became rather much filled with whiskey and tried to improve Lizzie's looks by using a razor. After hearing the case the judge fined the defendant $25 and costs.[51]

Most of the disciplinary problems were temporarily solved when in November 1890, the Twenty-fifth Infantry received orders to dispatch companies to participate in the last major Indian campaign to engage the United States Army. The Pine Ridge Campaign, as it was later designated, had its origins in the Ghost Dance movement, a new, messianic religion, which had attracted thousands of converts among the Plains Indians. The Ghost Dance movement recognized that the day of massive resistance against the white man had ended: now, it was time to turn from violence to dance and song. These dances, it was believed, would hasten the return of the buffalo and the withdrawal of the white men from the plains. When warriors began preparing shirts bearing secret symbols which, according to the Ghost Dancers, were to protect them from white men's bullets, the Indian agents began to fear trouble.[52] In November 1890 the army was placed on alert in case there should be a large-scale Indian uprising.

Major General Nelson A. Miles, commander of the Division of the Missouri, directed the overall campaign against the Sioux Ghost Dancers. As fear over the outbreak of a serious Indian war mounted, army units were rushed in from all over the West to the posts surrounding the Pine Ridge and Rosebud Indian reservations. It was a massive concentration of the army in the West. In response to orders, the Twenty-fifth sent four companies to Fort Keogh, the northwest operations center, on November 29, 1890, where they remained bivouacked under Sibley tents until the Pine Ridge campaign was concluded.[53] Winter at Fort Keogh proved severe with temperatures below freezing most of the time, and sometimes reaching nineteen degrees below zero.[54] The Twenty-fifth Infantry did not participate in any of the actual fighting, but acted as a reserve force for those engaged in the field.

The Pine Ridge campaign marked the end of the Indian wars. Once proud and defiant, the Plains Indians were now completely under the domination of the white men. The primary cause for the Indians' final surrender was the combination of cavalry and infantry which for many years had fought them in all kinds of weather and under a variety of circumstances. The Twenty-fifth Infantry, although it did not fire a rifle in anger during the Pine Ridge fighting, did have a part in this last campaign.

NOTES

1. U.S., Congress, House Executive Documents, *Annual Report of the Secretary of War, 1869–1870*, 41st Cong., 2d Sess., I, 24.

2. U.S., Congress, House Executive Documents, *Annual Report of the Secretary of War, 1869–1870*, 41st Cong., 2d Sess., I, 24.

3. General C. C. Augur to Assistant Adjutant General, Headquarters, Military Division of the Atlantic, March 17, 1879, Letters Received, Adjutant General's Office, File No. 1272, RG 94, NA.

4. Ibid.

5. Ibid., General William T. Sherman's endorsement to General Augur's letter, March 25, 1879.

6. Ibid., Secretary of War G. W. McCrary's endorsement to General Augur's letter, April 1, 1879.

7. Ibid., the Quartermaster General's endorsement to General William T. Shermans' endorsement, March 31, 1879.

8. Regimental Returns, Twenty-fifth Infantry Regiment, June, 1880, RG 94, NA.

9. Ibid., July, August, 1880, RG 94, NA.

10. Report of inspection of Fort Randall, Dakota Territory, October, 1881, Letters Received, Inspector General's Office, File No. 1262, RG 159, NA.

11. Captain R. P. Hughes to Adjutant General, Department of Dakota, Letters Received, Adjutant General's Office, October, 1883, RG 94, NA.

12. Ibid.

13. Report of inspection of Fort Meade, Dakota Territory, Letters Received, Inspector General's Office, File No. 718, 1880, RG 159, NA.

14. Ibid., File No. 1198, September, 1881, RG 159, NA.

15. Ibid., File No. 1019, 1887, RG 159, NA.

16. Post Returns, Fort Hale, Dakota Territory, November, 1880, RG 98, NA.

17. Post Returns, Fort Meade, Dakota Territory, July, August, 1883, RG 98, NA.

18. Ibid., May, June, October, 1881, RG 98, NA.

19. George E. Hyde, *A Sioux Chronicle*, pp. 75–76; W. Fletcher Johnson, *Life of Sitting Bull and History of the Indian War of 1890–91*, pp. 252–256; John C. Ewers, *The Blackfeet*, pp. 174–184.

20. Post Returns, Fort Randall, Dakota Territory, July, 1882, RG 98, NA.

21. Colonel George L. Andrews to Assistant Adjutant General of the Department of Dakota, September 20, 1881, Letters Sent, Fort Randall, Dakota Territory, RG 393, NA.

22. Johnson, *Life of Sitting Bull*, pp. 156–160; Hyde, *A Sioux Chronicle*, pp. 76–77.

23. Post Returns, Fort Randall, Dakota Territory, October, 1881, RG 98, NA.

24. Stanley Vestal, *New Sources of Indian History, 1850–1891*, p. 268.

25. Colonel George L. Andrews to Assistant Adjutant General of the Department of Dakota, Letters Sent, Fort Randall, Dakota Territory, September 26, 1881, RG 393, NA.

26. Post Returns, Fort Randall, Dakota Territory, May, 1883, RG 98, NA. Sitting Bull was killed in 1890 at Standing Rock Agency in an attempt by Indian police to place him under arrest.

27. Regimental Returns, Twenty-fifth Infantry Regiment, September, 1883, RG 94, NA.

28. Letter of C. S. Curtis to Lieutenant Colonel M. M. Blunt, Twenty-fifth Infantry Regiment, Scrapbook, United States Army Commands, Mobile, RG 391, NA; Regimental Returns, Twenty-fifth Infantry Regiment, September, 1883, RG 94, NA.

29. Regimental Returns, Twenty-fifth Infantry Regiment, June, August, 1884, RG 94, NA.

30. Letters Received, Adjutant General's Office, File No. 6443, 1885, RG 94, NA. This file contains a number of newspaper clippings concerning the events surrounding the shooting of Robert S. Bell, Dr. Lynch's death and the subsequent lynching of Corporal Hallon, as well as the official correspondence relating to the incident.

31. Ibid.

32. "I take it for granted that in the territory of Dakota the keeping of houses of ill-fame is prohibited by law, but, notwithstanding the law there are in the town, two brothels which would appear to have been established for the express purpose of catering to the taste and pandering to the passions of the colored troops, for they are "stocked" with colored prostitutes—negresses and mulattoes. They are, I am assured, places of the vilest character and it was at one of them that the affray of September 19th occurred. Had no such place existed it is most improbable that any affray would have occurred, and if the people of Sturgis City suffer such places to exist, they must, I submit, expect the natural result of their existence. . . . And I submit further that, until the people shall have surpressed these dens . . . they will not be in a position to ask the government to change its garrison." Ibid.

33. Reports of inspection of Fort Missoula, Montana Territory, Letters Received, Inspector General's Office, File No. 940, August, 1888; File No. 1257, August, 1889, RG 159, NA.

34. Colonel George L. Andrews to Assistant Adjutant General of the Department of Dakota, April 10, 1889, Letters Sent, Fort Missoula, Montana Territory, RG 393, NA.

35. "The garrison consists of the Headquarters, Band and four companies of the 25th Infantry and two medical officers: therefore quarters are required for seventeen officers; the post furnished but thirteen sets, consequently officers and their families are now quartered in attics and subject to such other reductions as seems best adapted to the convenience and comfort of all." Colonel George L. Andrews to Assistant Adjutant General of the Department of Dakota, Letters Sent, Fort Missoula, Montana, 1890, RG 393, NA.

36. *Great Falls Tribune* (Great Falls, Montana Territory) June 13, 1888.

37. The events preceding the lynching of Private Robert Robinson were reconstructed from accounts appearing in the *Great Falls Tribune*, June 13, 1888; *Missoula Gazette* (Missoula, Montana Territory), June 23, 1888; and the *Rising Sun* (Sun River, Montana Territory), June 13, 1888.

38. *Rising Sun*, June 13, 1888.

39. *Missoula Gazette*, June 2, 1888.

40. Ibid., June 30, 1888.

41. Colonel George L. Andrews to Mr. Williams, Helena, Montana Territory, July 22, 1888, Letters Sent, Missoula, Montana Territory, RG 393, NA.

42. *Missoula Gazette*, October 16, 1889.

43. Regimental Returns, Twenty-fifth Infantry Regiment, June, July, 1889, RG 94, NA.

44. Ibid., April, May, July, September, 1890, RG 94, NA; U.S. Congress, House Executive Documents, *Annual Report of the Secretary of War, 1890–1891*, 51st Cong., 2d Sess., II, 188–190; Post Returns, Fort Missoula, Montana, April, July, September, RG 98, NA.

45. Post Returns, Fort Missoula, Montana Territory, September, 1889, RG 98, NA.

46. Regimental Returns, Twenty-fifth Infantry Regiment,

September, 1890, RG 98, NA; Post Returns, Fort Shaw, Montana Territory, RG 98, NA.

47. Regimental Returns, Twenty-fifth Infantry Regiment, October, 1889, RG 94, NA.

48. Ibid., May, 1890, RG 94, NA.

49. Colonel George L. Andrews to Assistant Adjutant General of the Department of Dakota, March 12, 1889, Letters Sent, Fort Missoula, Montana Territory, RG 393, NA.

50. *Weekly Missoulian* (Missoula, Montana), November 6, 1889.

51. Ibid., December 11, 1889.

52. William T. Hagan, *American Indians*, pp. 130–134.

53. Regimental Returns, Twenty-fifth Infantry Regiment, November, December, 1890, January, February, 1891, RG 94, NA.

54. *Stock Growers Journal* (Miles City, Montana), December 27, 1890.

4

The

Twenty-fourth Infantry

in the Southwest

After ten years along the Rio Grande River, the Twenty-fourth Infantry was finally relieved of its border duty. In the fall of 1880 the regiment received orders transferring it to Indian Territory in present-day Oklahoma where it was to occupy three major army posts, Fort Reno, Fort Sill, and Fort Supply. One company was stationed at Fort Elliott in the Texas panhandle. By the end of December all companies of the regiment were garrisoned, with regimental headquarters located at Fort Supply.[1]

The officers and men of the Twenty-fourth had eagerly anticipated the change of stations. With the exception of Fort Elliott, they found that the posts were in better repair than those they had left in Texas. At Fort Sill the men had stone barracks equipped with heated baths and washrooms, and at Fort Supply the buildings and barracks were all in an excellent state of repair.[2] With living conditions thus improved, garrison life was much more pleasant.

But apart from living conditions, and possibly the climate, everything was about the same as it had been in

Texas. The men still performed the necessary guard and fatigue duties, including the off-post detail of constructing and repairing telegraph lines. One company, which left Fort Supply in August 1881 with orders to cut a thousand cedar poles, was in the field over two weeks cutting poles for the line that was to connect Fort Supply with Fort Dodge, Kansas.[3] Another company of the regiment was assigned the job of constructing the line. Lieutenant J. B. Batchelor left Fort Supply in September 1881 with a detail of twenty men to begin the work and remained in the field over two months before returning to the post.[4] As might be imagined, the job of digging holes, placing poles, and stringing wire across the plains of Indian Territory was not an enviable assignment.

Because Indian Territory was off limits to white settlers and travelers, the garrisons were more isolated than usual from civilization. The army had to build its own access roads to the posts, and what travel did occur in Indian Territory was restricted to official business with the army garrisons or Indian agencies. In 1887 Colonel Joseph H. Potter, the commanding officer of the Twenty-fourth Infantry, was asked by his department headquarters about the most expedient route to Fort Supply. He replied that it was best to travel by railroad to Dodge City, Kansas, and then to Fort Supply by stagecoach, adding that a new wagon road had just been completed from Fort Supply to Kiowa, Kansas.[5] Colonel Potter also informed the department that it was possible to reach Fort Elliott by a triweekly stagecoach from Fort Supply. The new wagon road Potter mentioned had been built by the men of the Twenty-fourth, and as events later proved, it was a fortunate thing for Fort Supply.[6] In September 1886 the stagecoach line between that post and Dodge City was abandoned. Another stage line using the new wagon road had started operations in July between Fort Supply and Kiowa, Kansas, and it provided the garrison's only regular contact with the outside world. It was an eighteen-hour trip from Kiowa to Fort Supply, and it was scheduled six days a week.[7] As a matter of military information, all roads connecting the various posts in Indian Territory were carefully described, the full particulars noted in reports compiled by the men of the Twenty-fourth.[8]

Earlier, Colonel Potter had described the garrison's isolated situation by saying, "The distance from this post [Fort Supply] to Fort Reno is one hundred and twenty miles, to Fort Elliott, Texas is ninety-two miles, to Dodge City, Kansas is seventy-four miles."[9] Although the officers and men were pleased by the change of scenery, they were disappointed at still being removed from civilization, and the remoteness caused problems. In Texas there were border towns the men could visit, but in Indian Territory there were no communities near the posts, and the isolation increased the need for off-duty recreation.

The post trader at Fort Supply provided a major source of off-duty amusement for the black soldiers. He dispensed food, drink, and light wine, but he was forbidden by law to sell hard liquor to the troops. He also maintained a billiards room, a favorite gathering place for the men. Consequently, when a fire struck the post trader's establishment, it was regarded by both officers and men as a major disaster.[10] The post trader, in the eyes of commanding officers, was an important contributor to the morale at every frontier fort. Colonel Z. R. Bliss of the Twenty-fourth wrote to the Adjutant General in Washington, requesting permission for the Southern Kansas Railroad to bring beer and light wine to Woodward, Indian Territory, which was the supply point.[11] The request was undoubtedly made so that the post trader would be assured of a replenished supply; normally, because they were not official army issue, the trader's supplies were brought in by wagon.

However, not all off-duty recreation enjoyed by the

men of the Twenty-fourth was under the auspices of the post trader: gambling, which was prohibited by army regulations, was nonetheless a popular pastime. Post records reveal several instances of men in the Twenty-fourth being court-martialed for gambling in or near their quarters.[12] Dice and card games such as casino, cribbage, and pinochle were probably the favorite barracks amusements.[13] Naturally, the one abiding off-duty interest common among all frontier soldiers was to seek out and enjoy female companionship.[14] Due to the restrictions prohibiting civilians from entering Indian Territory, the opportunities for the pleasures of female company were severely limited. One enterprising black civilian smuggled a white prostitute named Jennie Brown into Indian Territory, and at night he would bring her near the post so that she would be accessible to the troops. When the post commander discovered what was going on, he had Jennie escorted out of Indian Territory and warned her not to return. As she was being taken away, Jennie waved goodbye to the soldiers at the post trader's store and told them that she would be back in a couple of weeks.[15] Three months passed without a word from Jennie Brown, until she was discovered near the post disguised as a man and doing business as usual. This prompted Colonel Bliss to arrest Jennie and send her to Ashland, Kansas, to face federal charges for reentering Indian Territory.[16]

Army regulations during this period prohibited soldiers from marrying, with the exception of some enlisted men whose wives agreed to become servants for officers' families or laundresses for one of the companies on the post—an arrangement that was common in the Twenty-fourth Infantry. Living conditions for these women and their children were crude at best. The army neither provided for their housing nor assumed any responsibility for them; as a result, they were forced to live in whatever type of shelter they could find. Every soldier when he reenlisted signed a document acknowledging that the army would not be responsible for his wife or family, nor was his status as a married man to prevent him from being transferred as the needs of the service dictated.[17]

These arrangements were far from ideal and, on occasion, could become unpleasant for all concerned. For example, Lieutenant J. B. Batchelor, Jr., of the Twenty-fourth Infantry found himself in difficulty as the result of hiring a Private Alexander's wife to be his family servant. Batchelor had paid Mrs. Alexander's travel expenses from the East to Fort Supply with the understanding that she would work as a maid. One night the lieutenant was awakened by the loud and excited voice of Mrs. Alexander arguing with his wife. He went to the kitchen and ordered Mrs. Alexander to go to her tent, believing she was drunk. Later, Lieutenant Batchelor went to her tent and told her she was discharged. The following morning Mrs. Alexander begged the lieutenant to remain in the service of his family and Batchelor consented to keep her on the condition that she agree to see her husband only at specified times, since apparently she was spending too much time with her husband to the neglect of her maid's duties. Informed of the episode, Private Alexander angrily replied that he would take his wife away from the lieutenant's house. Batchelor then demanded that he have his wife out by noon that same day. As a result of the angry exchange, Private Alexander filed a complaint against Lieutenant Batchelor, and, though the charges were not sustained, the lieutenant was out the price of Mrs. Alexander's ticket to Fort Supply and the services of a maid.[18]

Notwithstanding the isolation of the posts and the rigors of duty, the Twenty-fourth Infantry had the lowest desertion rate of any regiment in the army during the years 1880 to 1886. This was particularly significant when contrasted with the rates of the other regiments sharing the same posts whose desertions were twenty to fifty times those of the Twenty-fourth.[19] The Third Cavalry, stationed in Indian Territory in 1885 and garrisoned with the Twenty-fourth, had 104 desertions that year and the Fifth Cavalry 99, while the Twenty-fourth recorded only 3 desertions.[20] This record was established during a period when desertion was the biggest single personnel problem the army faced.[21] In his annual report of 1882, Secretary of War Robert T. Lincoln noted that for every two soldiers who enlisted, one deserted.[22] Studies made to determine the causes of desertions disclosed that those units with good morale, discipline, and esprit de corps had the fewest desertions.[23] On this basis it would appear that the Twenty-fourth Infantry was the finest and best-disciplined regiment in the Army. Unfortunately, no one in authority drew this obvious conclusion, or if he noticed it, did not draw attention to it.

A combination of many factors had enabled the black infantry regiments to develop a strong esprit de corps, but most important was the fact that they were all-black regiments. There was a strong desire among the men to prove to the army, to society, and to themselves that they could soldier as well as white troops. They were particularly sensitive to any unfavorable publicity or comment about their regiment, as was evidenced by their response to the following incident. A sergeant and two privates of Company F of the Twenty-fourth Infantry left Fort Elliott, Texas, in 1885 as guards for two white soldiers who were being sent as prisoners to the military prison at Fort Leavenworth, Kansas. While their train was taking on water near Bellevue, Kansas, a band of robbers held it up. While one outlaw held the engineer and fireman captive, his accomplices went through the cars. When the outlaws reached the coach in which the three black guards and the prisoners were riding, they faced three pistols, drawn and cocked. At that point the sergeant told his men not to shoot and to lay down their pistols, fearing that an innocent bystander might be shot.[24]

Several newspapers, including some on the East Coast, reported the incident and censured the sergeant and the two privates for their failure to resist the robbers. Incensed over the unfavorable publicity that the Twenty-fourth, and black soldiers in general were receiving as a result of the incident, a number of men of Company F held a protest meeting at Fort Elliott under the leadership of their first sergeant and a corporal. They expressed their disgust and passed resolutions condemning the cowardly conduct of the sergeant and the two privates. Copies of their resolutions were sent to several newspapers for publication. Although both the first sergeant and the corporal were later court-martialed for holding an unauthorized meeting, their attitude was indicative of the pride and esprit de corps of the black infantry.[25]

The primary responsibility of the army in Indian Territory was to keep whites out and keep the Indians peaceful. The principal force for preventing the whites from crossing into Indian Territory was the cavalry, while the infantry was used to keep the peace at various Indian agencies. A typical instance occurred when Company F of the Twenty-fourth, along with all the available cavalry from Fort Sill, was ordered to the field to assist in discouraging a threatened Indian outbreak at the Anadarko Indian Agency. After the fear of the outbreak had subsided, another company of the Twenty-fourth Infantry was assigned temporarily to the agency at the request of the Indian agent.[26]

In the spring of 1888, General Philip H. Sheridan recommended to Secretary of War W. C. Endicott that the Twenty-fourth Infantry be moved to the Department of Arizona to relieve the Thirteenth Infantry, which had been there since 1880.[27] The Twenty-fourth received orders for

the transfer in May 1888, and by June the move was completed. The regiment was garrisoned at Fort Apache, Fort
Grant, Fort Thomas, and San Carlos Indian Agency, all of
which were in Arizona Territory. Headquarters for the
regiment was established at Fort Bayard, New Mexico
Territory. The men discovered the living conditions at
their new posts were much worse than those they had enjoyed in Indian Territory. In fact, the garrison at San
Carlos was changed every six months to prevent a breakdown in the troops' health and morale. The temperature
at San Carlos in July was often 110 degrees in the shade
and on some occasions as high as 118 degrees. General A.
McCook, commander of the Department of Arizona, reported in 1891 that he considered it almost inhuman to ex-
pose troops to such discomfort.[28] After a visit to San
Carlos, Frederic Remington, the artist, wrote:

> The San Carlos reservation . . . is a vast tract of
> desert and mountains, and near the center of it, on
> the Gila River, is a great flat plain where the long
> low adobe buildings of the agency are built. Lines of
> white tents belonging to the cantonment form a
> square to the north. I arrived at this place one even-
> ing after a hot and tiresome march, in company with
> a cavalry command. . . . The San Carlos is a hotter
> place than I ever intend to visit again. A man who
> is used to breathing the fresh air of New York Bay
> is in no condition to enjoy at one and the same time
> the dinner and the turkish bath which accompanies
> it.[29]

The barracks at Fort Thomas were in a miserable
state: the floors rotten, the roofs leaky, many of the win-
dows broken out, and the adobe walls cracked and crum-
bling.[30] At Fort Apache the men found their barracks in
fair condition on the inside but the outside was in desperate
need of repair.[31] Fort Grant was in a similar state of disre-

pair; in addition, there were no bathing facilities on post.[32] Of all the forts, Bayard was in the best condition, although the barracks were overcrowded.[33] At Fort Bayard, as at most frontier posts, the officers and noncommissioned officers were quartered in overcrowded and inferior housing; and as usual, there was a shortage of housing for the families of noncommissioned officers. The post quartermaster at Fort Bayard offered to set up five hospital tents and eleven worn wall tents to be used as temporary quarters. Z. R. Bliss, the regimental commander, requested approval for the use of the tents as recommended by the post quartermaster, but the department commander denied the request.[34] Colonel R. P. Hughes in the Quartermaster General's report for 1890 drew attention to the substandard conditions, stating that something should be done to relieve the situation of married soldiers: the children of these soldiers, living in sheds and shanties, suffered from exposure to the elements as well as a poor diet. The sanitary conditions of these quarters, he related, are the source of much disease and sickness among the enlisted men's families.[35] In short, housing for the married soldier of the Twenty-fourth was as inadequate in the Department of Arizona as it had been in Texas or in Indian Territory.

During the Arizona years the Twenty-fourth was not in the field as much as it had been in the past, although the companies did engage in the usual practice marches and bivouacs specified by the Department of Arizona.[36] To maintain combat readiness the black soldiers would march out to the field with full field equipment on their backs.[37] The practice marches not only increased the field proficiency of the companies, they provided physical conditioning for the men. At the same time, because the cavalry was out in the field most of the time, the infantry was again occupied with the basic duties of running a frontier post. Thus repair and construction work was the usual fare for the infantrymen at these posts.[38]

The monotony of garrison duty in New Mexico and Arizona, due to the oppressive climate and surroundings, and the routine of duty, caused a marked increase in the restlessness of the men. The records show that many of the enlisted men had an increased propensity to consume alcohol and occasionally men were found drinking in their barracks during off-duty hours. In some instances, barracks drinking, which was strictly forbidden by army regulations, would result in a fight.[39] Men were found drunk on duty or creating a drunken disturbance. Private Richard Cox of Company D of the Twenty-fourth became drunk while on a sawmill detail and attacked a Private Lambert with a hatchet. Fortunately, Cox was restrained and the hatchet taken from him; then, without warning, he again attacked Lambert, this time inflicting knife wounds. Cox surrendered and was placed under arrest, but only after being threatened with a pistol.[40]

The men of the Twenty-fourth managed to obtain whiskey despite the regimental commander's best attempts to limit its use. Toward the close of President Rutherford B. Hayes' administration an army-wide abstinence policy was introduced; however, in the mid-1880s the abstinence policy was relaxed so as to allow beer and light wine to be sold by the post traders.[41] Since the sale or consumption of hard liquor was not allowed on post, the men often bought "rot gut" at the numerous "whiskey ranches" or "hog ranches," as they were sometimes called, that sprang up near the forts. A whiskey ranch usually consisted of a crude building with a bar that dispensed cheap whiskey and beer. On paydays, gamblers and prostitutes following the trail of the army paymaster, would descend upon the ranches to play their respective trades. The regimental commander of the Twenty-fourth was concerned about the whiskey ranches near the posts because of the vices they spawned. His concern was supported by the observations of the post surgeon at Fort Grant who reported a direct relationship between the whiskey ranches and venereal disease.[42]

Problems with off-post drinking increased at Fort Bayard in 1889 to such an extent that Colonel Z. R. Bliss was obliged to request permission for the post trader to sell beer and light wine. Noting that the town of Central City, New Mexico, was only one mile from the fort, Bliss stated that its principal reason for existence was to furnish saloons and houses of prostitution for the men of the Twenty-fourth Infantry. The Colonel argued that he would be able to keep more men on post, under supervision, and thereby prevent many minor disturbances if the post trader were allowed to sell light alcoholic beverages.[43]

Off-post drinking had been a problem for post commanders in the West for nearly two decades and was the subject of serious study by the army. Canteens were established with the idea of providing a clean, wholesome, government-owned place for men to go on their off-duty time. By supplying an alternative to the whiskey ranches and town saloons, the army hoped to direct the mens' energies into more constructive activities. The advent of the canteen was welcomed by most post commanders, officers, and post surgeons in garrisons throughout the West.[44] Its influence on the men of the Twenty-fourth stationed at Fort Grant, Arizona, was definitely positive. The post surgeon there reported the improvement in 1889: "Since the opening of the canteen and bowling alley the men have visited the whiskey ranches less frequently, as they have had the means of amusing themselves when off duty without resorting to these dens."[45]

Of course not all the men of the Twenty-fourth spent their free time carousing and whoring, but, for the most part, exhibited a wide range of interests and activities. Some produced theatrical performances for the post residents, while others arranged minstrel shows that were performed off post for civilian audiences.[46] Some found the post reading room a quiet place to read and escape the noise of barracks life. Army reports reveal that a large number of the officers and men read the current magazines, newspapers, and books available to them. Chaplain Allen Allensworth, the regimental chaplain, sponsored a literary and debating society which met once a week after duty hours in the school in an attempt to stimulate some intellectual interests in the men.[47] Fort Bayard was fortunate in having a well-equipped gymnasium and baseball facilities.[48] Fort Grant had a gymnasium, library, billiard tables, and two bowling alleys that were in almost constant use.[49] In addition, each post had men engaged in a variety of sports and hobbies.[50] Occasionally a traveling theatrical company or a specialty act would perform for the troops. In 1890 Willis Stanley offered to provide a balloon ascension and theatrical production for the garrison at Fort Bayard one Sunday afternoon. Colonel Bliss, the post commander, granted permission for the balloon ascension but refused consent for the theatrical performance because it was Sunday.[51] These varied interests and activities in which the men of the Twenty-fourth participated belied the stereotyped image of the frontier soldier as a drunkard and whoremonger.

The Twenty-fourth Infantry continued to perform escort duties as it had done for nearly two decades of frontier service. It was in discharge of such duty that members of the Twenty-fourth were recommended for the Congressional Medal of Honor for conspicuous heroism. The occasion involved an army paymaster who was traveling between Fort Grant and Fort Thomas in Arizona on May 11, 1889, under the protective escort of two noncommissioned officers and nine privates of the Tenth Cavalry and Twenty-fourth Infantry. Suddenly a large boulder appeared in the middle of the road; the troops dismounted and, except for a few left guarding the wagon, went with Sergeant Benjamin Brown to assist in removing the obstacle. As the soldiers approached the large rock, a voice from the top of a nearby ledge called to them to put their hands up. Almost immediately a shot rang out, followed by a volley of rifle fire from a ridge near the pay wagon. The first man hit was the pay wagon driver. Two of the horses pulling the wagon were also shot making it impossible for the wagon to move. Then the highwaymen began picking off the escort one by one.

Although Sergeant Brown was caught in the open with the rest of his men and was shot in the abdomen during the first volley, he continued to fight. Eight men of the eleven-man escort were wounded, all of whom fought until the situation forced them to retreat to a nearby creek bed. After they withdrew, fifteen to twenty robbers came down from the ridge and took the money from the pay wagon. Meanwhile, Corporal Isaiah Mayes, in spite of his wounds, struggled two miles to Cottonwood Ranch to fetch help for his comrades. By the time assistance arrived the bandits had left, taking with them $28,345.10.[52] Major Wham, in his official report of the fight, was full of praise for the conduct of his escort: "I served in the infantry during the entire Civil War and served in sixteen major battles, but I never witnessed better courage or better fighting than shown by these colored soldiers."[53] The major recommended nine of the escort for the Medal of Honor. As a result, seven privates received certificates of merit and the two noncommissioned officers received the Medal of Honor.[54]

At the conclusion of the Indian wars in 1891, the Twenty-fourth Infantry was still on duty in the Southwest. Like its sister regiment, the Twenty-fifth, it had compiled an impressive record of service under the difficult and demanding conditions of the frontier. The Twenty-fourth had maintained the lowest desertion rate of any regiment in the army and, as in the case of the other black regiments in the regular army, its court-martial rate was lower than most white regiments. In one of the rare instances of official recognition, the Secretary of War in 1889 paid tribute to the record of the black soldiers by saying, "There are now two regiments of infantry and two of cavalry of colored men, and their record for good service is excellent. They are neat, orderly, and obedient, are seldom brought before court-martial, and rarely desert."[55]

NOTES

1. Post Returns, Fort Supply, Indian Territory, December, 1880, Record Group 98, National Archives (hereafter abbreviated as RG and NA); U.S., Congress, House Executive Documents, *Annual Report of the Secretary of War, 1881–1882*, 47th Cong., 1st Sess., II, 50.

2. Report of inspection of Fort Supply, Indian Territory, Letters Received, Inspector General's Office, File No. 1001, 1886; File No. 1003, 1887; Report of Inspection of Fort Sill, Indian Territory, Letters Received, Inspector General's Office, File No. 1303, 1887; File No. 1003, 1887. All the preceding in RG 159, NA.

3. Post Returns, Fort Supply, Indian Territory, August, 1881, RG 98, NA.

4. Ibid., September, November, 1881, RG 98, NA.

5. Colonel Joseph H. Potter to Assistant Adjutant General, Department of the Missouri, August 20, 1885, Letters Sent, Fort Supply, Indian Territory, RG 393, NA.

6. Colonel Joseph H. Potter to Assistant Adjutant General, Department of the Missouri, August 18, 1885, Letters Sent, Fort Supply, Indian Territory, RG 393, NA.

7. Colonel Z. R. Bliss to Paymaster General, Washington, D.C., November 4, 1886, Letters Sent, Fort Supply, Indian Territory, RG 393, NA.

8. Colonel Z. R. Bliss to Assistant Adjutant General, Department of the Missouri, January, 1887, Letters Sent, Fort

Supply, Indian Territory, RG 393, NA. These reports included a description of the countryside, road conditions, river crossings, availability of fresh water, wood supply, and the quantity of grazing grass.

9. Colonel Joseph H. Potter to Assistant Adjutant General Department of the Missouri, March 3, 1884, Letters Sent, Fort Supply, Indian Territory, RG 393, NA.

10. Post Returns, Fort Supply, Indian Territory, February, 1882, RG 98, NA.

11. Colonel Z. R. Bliss to Adjutant General, Washington, D.C., July 13, 1887, Letters Sent, Fort Supply, Indian Territory, RG 393, NA.

12. Post Adjutant to Commanding Officer, Company H, Twenty-fourth Infantry, January 4, 1888, Letters Sent, Fort Supply, Indian Territory, RG 393, NA.

13. See Don Rickey, Jr., *Forty Miles a Day on Beans and Hay*, p. 209.

14. Ibid., pp. 168–170.

15. Colonel Z. R. Bliss to Assistant Adjutant General, Department of the Missouri, April 17, 1887, Letters Sent, Fort Supply, Indian Territory, RG 393, NA.

16. Colonel Z. R. Bliss to U.S. Commissioner, Ashland, Kansas, July 10, 1887, Letters Sent, Fort Supply, Indian Territory, RG 393, NA.

17. These documents are found in a number of files from the Adjutant General's Office in RG 94, NA.

18. Lieutenant J. B. Batchelor, Jr., endorsement of letter from Commanding Officer requesting information regarding the difficulties with Mrs. Alexander, May 4, 1883, Letters Sent, Fort Supply, Indian Territory, RG 393, NA.

19. U.S., Congress, House Executive Documents, *Annual Report of the Secretary of War, 1889–1890*, 51st Cong., 1st Sess., II, 83.

20. U.S., Congress, House Executive Documents, *Annual Report of the Secretary of War, 1885–1886*, 49th Cong., 1st Sess., II, 100.

21. Rickey, *Forty Miles a Day*, p. 144.

22. U.S., Congress, House Executive Documents, *Annual*

Report of the Secretary of War, 1882–1883, 47th Cong., 2d Sess., II, v.

23. U.S., Congress, House Executive Documents, *Annual Report of the Secretary of War, 1885–1886,* pp. 114–116.

24. Letters, newspaper clippings, and official comments related to the train robbery are in Letters Received, Adjutant General's office, File No. 6805, 1886, RG 94, NA.

25. Ibid., From report of the commanding officer at Fort Elliott, Texas, January 19, 1887.

26. U.S., Congress, House Executive Documents, *Annual Report of the Secretary of War, 1887–1888,* 50th Cong., 1st Sess., II, 149.

27. General Philip H. Sheridan to Secretary of War W. C. Endicott, April 5, 1888, Letters Sent, Headquarters, United States Army, RG 94, NA.

28. U.S., Congress, House Executive Documents, *Annual Report of the Secretary of War, 1891–1892,* 52d Cong., 1st Sess., II, 260.

29. Harold McCracken, ed., *Frederic Remington's Own West,* pp. 28–29.

30. Report of Inspection of Fort Thomas, Arizona, Letters Received, Inspector General's Office, File No. 1296, 1889, RG 159, NA.

31. Report of inspection of Fort Apache, Arizona, Letters Received, Inspector General's Office, File No. 963, 1888, RG 159, NA.

32. Report of inspection of Fort Grant, Arizona, Letters Received, Inspector General's Office, File No. 974, 1889, RG 159, NA.

33. Colonel Z. R. Bliss to Assistant Adjutant General, Department of Arizona, January 25, 1890, Letters Sent, Fort Bayard, New Mexico, RG 393, NA.

34. Colonel A. R. Bliss endorsement of Post Quartermaster's request, June 19, 1888, Letters Sent, Fort Bayard, New Mexico, RG 393, NA.

35. U.S., Congress, House Executive Documents, *Annual Report of the Secretary of War, 1890–1891,* 51st Cong., 2d Sess., II, 101.

36. Post Returns, Fort Bayard, New Mexico, November, 1888, RG 98, NA.

37. Ibid., October, 1889, RG 98, NA.

38. Colonel Z. R. Bliss to Assistant Adjutant General, Department of Arizona, November 22, 1888, Letters Sent, Fort Bayard, New Mexico, RG 393, NA.

39. Colonel Z. R. Bliss to Assistant Adjutant General, Department of Arizona, November 17, 1888, Letters Sent, Fort Bayard, New Mexico, RG, 393, NA.

40. Colonel Z. R. Bliss to Assistant Adjutant General, Department of Arizona, December 28, 1888, Letters Sent, Fort Bayard, New Mexico, RG 393, NA.

41. Rickey, *Forty Miles a Day*, pp. 168–169.

42. "During the last six months venereal diseases have prevailed at this post and its vicinity to such an extent as to be almost epidemic. Most of the cases at the post have been contracted at the two whiskey ranches located just beyond the limits of the reservation, where a crowd of gamblers and prostitutes, who follow in the wake of the paymaster, congregate every two months to prey upon the enlisted men." *Annual Report of the Secretary of War, 1889–1890,* p. 849.

43. Colonel Z. R. Bliss to Assistant Adjutant General, Department of Arizona, December 2, 1889, Letters Sent, Fort Bayard, New Mexico, RG 393, NA.

44. Rickey, *Forty Miles a Day*, pp. 202–203; *Annual Report of the Secretary of War, 1891–1892*, pp. 66–76. The Secretary of War's report gives the army's views on the merits of the canteen. The post canteen was the grandfather of the present-day post exchange which is an established service on all army posts.

45. *Annual Report of the Secretary of War, 1889–1890,* p. 849.

46. Commanding Officer's endorsement of request for permission to allow the regimental band to accompany a regimental minstrel troupe playing an engagement in Silver City, New Mexico, June 22, 1888, Letters Sent, Fort Bayard, New Mexico, RG 393, NA.

47. Chaplain Allen Allensworth to Colonel Z. R. Bliss,

March 15, 1890, Letters Sent, Fort Bayard, New Mexico, RG 393, NA.

48. Report of inspection of Fort Bayard, New Mexico, Letters Received, Inspector General's Office, File No. 241, 1890, RG 159, NA.

49. Report of inspection of Fort Grant, Arizona, Letters Received, Inspector General's Office, File No. 240, 1890, RG 159, NA.

50. The men stationed at frontier posts engaged in a number of sports and games which included fishing, hunting, horseshoe pitching, foot racing, and boxing. The black regiments were particularly noted for their singing. See Rickey, *Forty Miles a Day*, pp. 186–189

51. Colonel Z. R. Bliss to Willis Stanley, Silver City, New Mexico, August 29, 1890, Letters Sent, Fort Bayard, New Mexico, RG 393, NA.

52. *Annual Report of the Secretary of War, 1889–1890*, 185; Irvin H. Lee, *Negro Medal of Honor Men*, pp. 78–80.

53. Lee, *Negro Medal of Honor Men*, pp. 79–80.

54. Ibid.

55. *Annual Report of the Secretary of War, 1889–1890*, p. 5.

5

The Black Infantry and Education in the Army

An army act of July 1866 specified that a chaplain was to be assigned to each black regiment. In addition to his regular religious duties, the chaplain was to be responsible for an educational program. This provision was unique because army chaplains were normally assigned to an entire post rather than to an individual regiment.[1] The army's involvement in the education of black soldiers grew out of the circumstances of the Civil War. As the freed slaves, or contrabands as they were called, fled into the Union lines and followed in the wake of the advancing army, the need arose for a program to feed them and prepare them for a life as free men and women. An important part of the program was teaching these freedmen to read and write, often under the supervision of the chaplains of the Union Army.[2] Later, as black regiments were formed in the Union Army, educational societies of the North sent teachers to the training camps to set up schools for the men.[3] But, again, much of the educational work in these black regiments was assigned to the chaplains. A colonel in the

Fifty-ninth U.S. Colored Infantry Regiment wrote his
son in 1863 that during off-duty hours the men were taught
by the chaplain and his wife to read and write.[4] The wife
of the colonel of the Thirty-fifth U.S. Colored Infantry
Regiment stated that the regimental chaplain assisted her
in teaching the men reading and writing.[5]

By 1866 the use of chaplains as educators in black
regiments was an accepted practice. During the early years
of Reconstruction, the development of an education program for freed blacks was sponsored by educational societies, religious denominations, and other benevolent groups
under the supervision of the Freedmen's Bureau.[6] In some
areas of the South, army chaplains were detailed as assistant
superintendents of education for the Freedmen's Bureau.[7]
Because of the role chaplains had played in the education
of black soldiers during the Civil War, the army in 1866
made the assignment of a regimental chaplain mandatory
for all black regiments.

The first chaplain of the Twenty-fourth Infantry was
the Reverend John N. Schultz, who served as regimental
chaplain from November 11, 1869 until July 23, 1875.
Schultz had previously served as the first and only chaplain
for the Thirty-eighth Infantry in Kansas and New Mexico
until that regiment was consolidated with the Forty-first
Infantry to become the Twenty-fourth. During those early
years on the Texas frontier, Schultz established and conducted a school for enlisted men.[8] He maintained his educational work with the black infantry until his resignation
in 1875.[9]

Chaplain D. Elington Barr, the first regimental chaplain of the Twenty-fifth Infantry, was particularly energetic in his conduct of the regiment's educational program.
Early reports indicate that he started conducting a school
for enlisted men while the regiment was stationed at Jackson Barracks, Louisiana, and that he even held additional
classes in his quarters after duty hours for those unable to

attend during the day.[10] Chaplain Barr continued to develop an educational program for the men of the regiment under the trying conditions of the Texas posts. He remained with the regiment until forced to resign his commission in September 1872 for questionable reasons.[11] When news of his resignation became known, he received a letter of appreciation from the Department of Education of the State of Texas for his work in the field of public education.[12] These early chaplains began a program of education in the black infantry that was to continue to grow throughout the regiments' service in the West.

In the early years in Texas, the primitive conditions severely hampered the chaplains' activities. Chaplain Barr reported from Fort Clark in 1871 that, lacking a proper building, the post school was conducted in the stable or the kitchen during inclement weather; in fair weather the school was held in the open air. Because of the many demands made upon them the men were unable to attend school regularly. A number of the men did not come, he believed, because of the inadequate school facilities.[13] In addition to devising a curriculum of study and teaching enlisted men, the chaplain was also obliged to conduct a school for the children of the post. For lack of a schoolroom, Chaplain Barr held classes for both the children and the men in his own quarters.[14]

Chaplain George Gatewood Mullins, who was destined to make a significant contribution to army education in general and to the education of the black infantry in particular, reported for duty at Fort Davis, Texas, on April 30, 1875.[15] Perhaps more than any one man, Chaplain Mullins pioneered the program of army education as it is known and practiced today. A minister of the Disciples of Christ Church, with a degree from the University of Kentucky, he brought with him a sense of dedication and perspicacity that made an important difference in the regiment as well as the army.[16] At the outset of his career with the Twenty-fifth Infantry Chaplain Mullins was not overjoyed with what he found. In fact, he was discouraged and cynical about the prospects of teaching black soldiers.

> They who sentimentally contend that there is no reason why the colored soldier should be considered inferior to the white; not only overlook the God-made differences of races, but do ignore all that is loudly claimed for the influence of freedom, education and society.
>
> I find these colored soldiers of the 25th Inf. Reg. and 10th Cav., generally of that abject servile disposition which does just what is absolutely necessary, and nothing more:—eye servants driven to duty by no praiseworthy pride, but fear of punishment.[17]

And the chaplain's misgivings were not alleviated when he observed the miserable condition of the school facility and its equipment.[18]

The regiment had been without a chaplain for almost three years; as a result, Mullins found himself having to re-establish the whole education program. His first step was to reopen the post school. The school quickly had an average daily attendance of eighty men, but the chaplain found that half of the students were just beginning to learn to read and write. None of them, he discovered, were beyond the level of the fourth grade. Chaplain Mullins began holding three school sessions every day of the week except Saturday and Sunday. In addition to the post school, the chaplain conducted a Sunday school, a Sunday morning worship service, and a preaching service in the evening.[19] The magnitude of the task before him plus the primitive conditions under which he had to work, led Chaplain Mullins to consider resigning.[20] But his energetic, thorough nature overcame his discouragement, and he determined to do the job. An inspector at Fort Davis in 1875 was so impressed by the work of Mullins that he declared, "I have no hesitation in saying that Chaplain Mullins is one of the most energetic, reasonable and serviceable of his profession in the army, that I have met in my inspections."[21]

As time passed, Mullins was heartened and moved by the enthusiasm and competitive spirit exhibited by the black soldiers in their school work.[22] The desire to read and write was a strong motivation among the enlisted men, who took great pride in mastering even simple sentences. At times, their fervor amounted to almost religious commitment.[23] Seeking to exploit this enthusiasm Mullins encouraged the company officers to stimulate greater participation in the educational programs among the men. Chaplain Mullins later reported that he and the officers succeeded in arousing in the ranks an ambition to learn that almost amounted to "comic furor."[24]

In his work with the black soldiers at Fort Davis, Chaplain Mullins observed a correlation between educational activity and good discipline. In one of his early reports he commented on the fact that approximately ten percent of the command was in the guard house. This and other problems led him to conclude that there was little to commend the black man for military life.[25] A year later, however, he was able to discern a change in the conduct of the men which he related directly to education. Mullins had approached education as something more than a process for teaching men to read and write; in his eyes it was a way to lead soldiers to a better moral life.[26] In a period of fifteen months he became so convinced of the relationship of good discipline and morality to education that in his report of a visit to Fort Bliss, Texas, he requested that a chaplain be assigned to that post, "For the sake of the moral and mental welfare of our poor men since a good Post School, and regular Divine service act powerfully to keep men out of the guard house and from courts martial, and particularly help develop a higher type soldier."[27]

Chaplain Mullins was beginning to articulate the ideas that were to make him a leading advocate of the social and military value of education in the army. Perhaps because he was a chaplain, he was able to see the social implications of a good army educational program. Certainly at the heart of the black soldiers' enthusiasm, Mullins sensed a fierce determination to be free citizens in a free society. The black soldiers were convinced that education was the key to social equality and acceptance. While at Fort Davis Chaplain Mullins observed:

> The ambition to be all that soldiers should be is not confined to a few of these sons of an unfortunate race. They are possessed of the notion that the colored people of the whole country are more or less affected by their conduct in the army. The chaplain is sometimes touched by evidence of their manly anxiety to be well thought of at Army HQ and throughout the states. This is the bottom secret of their patient toil, and surprising progress in the effort to get at least an elementary education.[28]

Chaplain Mullins believed that with education came a sense of self-respect, dignity, and achievement. He also had the wisdom to recognize that the army was the one agency in the country that could provide such an opportunity to a large number of young men.[29] It was in the spirit of this conviction that he sought to bring as many men as possible into his school program.

Chaplain Mullins approached his work as educator and teacher with the same dedication he brought to his ministerial duties—ultimately, their goals were little different. Out of a desire to do the job properly, he spent long hours in study and preparation. After the first year he normally held two sessions of school each day, the first in the afternoon and the second at night after duty hours.[30] The afternoon period included the children of the post and a few enlisted men, while the evening classes were devoted entirely to enlisted men. Weather and the misfortunes of frontier life often hindered his program, as on one occasion when a heavy downpour caused the chapel's sod roof to cave in and ruin the schoolroom. Though forced to suspend school for several weeks, so strong was the desire for education, he reported, that during the time the school was closed over 100 men kept their books with them and studied on their own in the barracks at night.[31]

Supposedly, education in the army was on a voluntary basis. There were no regulations which a commander could use to compel the illiterate soldier to attend school. However, Colonel George L. Andrews, commanding officer at Fort Clark, required all noncommissioned officers to attend the post school. He believed a sergeant should at least know how to read and write in order to perform minimal administrative duties.[32] But, since schooling was usually on a voluntary basis, Chaplain Mullins was forced to rely on the power of persuasion to attract most of the men into the school program, and he was continually exhorting them to enroll for their own self-improvement. Enlisted men, encouraged to stimulate interest among their comrades in the barracks, became Mullins' co-recruiters: "I have now among the men over twenty earnest coadjutors, who make it their daily care to exhort their comrades to quit whiskey and cards—to keep out of the Guard House, to study their books—attend church etc."[33]

The curriculum used in the post school included readings, writing, basic mathematics, history, and elementary science, with a flexible program to meet the varying levels of educational development of the enlisted men. Every Friday evening the chaplain would give a short lecture to those enrolled in the school on some topic of common civil, military, or moral law.[34]

For nearly three years he conducted the educational program by himself, until January 1878 when a sergeant was assigned to assist him. Earlier he had used some of the brighter scholars as classroom tutors for the slower students. For its first four years the chaplain's post school averaged over a hundred men a day.[35] Mullins' educational philosophy was simple but, under the circumstances, effective: "The great aim is to keep every man cheerfully busy every moment, and to make each man feel that much good is expected of him."[36]

The strain of his work, the demands made upon him as both chaplain and teacher, and the hardships of the frontier soon had its effect on Chaplain Mullins. Instructing men who had not been exposed to formal schooling, together with poor teaching conditions and primitive equipment, was a great emotional and physical drain. Late in 1875, Mullins, in a despondent mood, reported that he could find very little satisfaction in estimating what the "fruits of his labors would be for God and country" at Fort Davis, Texas.[37] In the course of his duties as a clergyman, the chaplain made regular visits to the sick in their quarters or in the post hospital, and if a death occurred on post he was called upon to officiate at the funeral service. His Sunday schedule was filled with activities from morning till night, and he officiated at all marriages and baptisms on post. As chaplain he was also concerned with the drinking habits of the men, which prompted him to organize a temperance society in January 1876. A short time later he reported that over sixty men had joined the society, all of whom had previously been heavy drinkers.[38]

The many activities, duties, and demands, plus the poor health of his wife, prompted Chaplain Mullins in 1877 to request a transfer from the Texas frontier to the East. The frustrations of a frontier chaplain were revealed in the five reasons he gave for wanting the transfer. First, he listed his inability to gain satisfaction in the vaguely defined position of regimental chaplain. The second reason he offered was the meager pay in relation to the demanding responsibilities placed upon him: the cost of frontier living was high, particularly for a family man. His third reason dealt with his personal ambitions; still a young man, he wanted to accomplish more than the limited opportunities of the frontier afforded. His wife's poor health was given as a fourth reason and was probably the actual stimulus in requesting the transfer. Finally, pointing to his record of service with the Twenty-fifth Infantry, particularly as teacher at the post school, he believed that he had done as much as a person could do under the circumstances, and now it was time for a change.[39]

Chaplain Mullins' petition for transfer was turned down on the basis that appointments as regimental chaplain could not be transferred to a post chaplaincy without being reappointed by the President. And since there were no positions as post chaplain vacant at the time, to apply for reappointment would be fruitless.[40] Under these circumstances outlined by the Adjutant General, Chaplain Mullins elected to stay with the Twenty-fifth as its chaplain and continue his work with the black soldiers.

A year later, in 1878, the War Department issued an order which required all posts, garrisons, and permanent camps to establish a school for enlisted men—an important step forward for education in the army. Previously, schools were an optional service provided by the individual post; an exception were the forts where black regiments were stationed. There, chaplains were required to maintain an educational program. The War Department further specified that the Quartermaster's Department was to be responsible for the construction of schoolrooms, libraries, reading rooms, and chapels, at the various installations and was to supply them with chairs, tables, desks, lamps, and bookshelves, in addition to the necessary fuel. By far the most significant aspect of the new order was that it instituted a definite means for giving financial support to the schools. According to the new order the post schools were to be maintained by post funds supplied by a ten cent tax levied monthly on the post trader for every officer or enlisted man serving at that particular fort.[41] Thus the Quartermaster's Department assumed responsibility for the buildings and the post funds were to be spent for books and instructional material. The War Department specified that the books used by the enlisted men and their children were to be purchased by the school, but officers' children and the children of civilians attending classes were expected to purchase their own books.[42]

The order, progressive in many respects, was deficient in two major areas. It did not provide for compulsory education of the uneducated enlisted men, nor did it provide for the hiring of trained school teachers. The question of compulsory education for soldiers continued to be a matter of controversy for a number of years. Many officers reasoned that compelling enlisted men to attend school not only violated their rights, but would cause widespread discontent and even prompt some to desert.[43] The omission of an authorization to hire trained school teachers reflected the army's reluctance to commit itself financially to a large-scale education program. It was the lack of qualified teachers that continued to be the weakest link in the system of army education.[44]

The army's official recognition of the necessity of supporting a school for enlisted men and children of the post gave Chaplain Mullins new encouragement. He continued in his determination to prove the social and military value of army education and to make schooling mandatory for illiterate soldiers. His official correspondence shows that he was firm in his conviction that education and morality had a noticeable effect on discipline. When classes were dismissed during the months of July and August in 1878 because of hot weather, Mullins reported that he observed a distinct increase in drinking and gambling among the men.[45] In December of the same year, he reported that he could discern a definite decrease in the number of soldiers in the guardhouse because the number of men enrolled in the school had increased.[46] He also wrote in 1878, with understandable pride, that in the past three years over 160 men who had not known the abc's when they first entered the school had been taught to read and write. Chaplain Mullins was particularly proud of the fact that twenty-four men from his school had been assigned as clerks in the regiment.[47] The lack of enlisted men in the black infantry who could perform clerical duties had been a constant complaint of the officers for years.[48] But more important, Mullins saw the educational program as a vehicle for developing self-respect and pride in the black soldiers.

> Camp followers—vulture gamblers, and dram sellers piteously complain of hard times, and do most cordially curse "how we do!" Indeed in the whole Regiment there is a growing and helpful Esprit de corps. . . . The soldiers are learning the high duty and privilege of holding themselves in respect, that others may respect them. They have aroused to an avowed ambition to align themselves not a whit behind any troops in the service.[49]

The record of accomplishment of Chaplain Mullins' educational program did not go unnoticed. General E. O. C. Ord, the commander of the Department of Texas, reported to higher headquarters: "The success of Chaplain Mullins with the schools—shows earnest and persevering attention and deserves commendation."[50] Mullins had demonstrated that a well-organized and adequately supported educational program had a beneficial influence on an army garrison, and that a correlation existed between good discipline and education.

In recognition of his success and interest in the field of army education, Chaplain Mullins was ordered on detached duty to act as assistant to General A. McCook, Chief of Education in the army. His first assignment was to devise a system which would organize all post schools on a similar basis; he was also to see that reading rooms and libraries were established at all army garrisons and furnished with reading materials. Mullins began a program for the standardization of education in the army that was to continue for several years. As a reward for his efforts Chaplain Mullins was appointed Chief of Education in the army on April 4, 1881. As head of the army's educational program he initiated additional policies to upgrade the quality of army education at the post level, and continued his plea for a corps of trained professional teachers. As Chief of Education, Mullins not only lobbied in Congress for stronger army education bills but engineered the passage of all significant legislation enhancing the stature and quality of education in the army. Mullins later said that he "was led by two Presidents and three Secretarys of War—ardently to study to make myself a worthy specialist in the subject of education."[51] His interest in education prompted him to write extensively on the subject during his tenure as Chief of Education.[52] Through his leadership a beginning was made in the standardization of textbooks and subject matter in post schools. Inspectors were ordered to include the post school and its facilities in their reports, and eventually each geographical department in the army was required to make an annual report on the situation at each post school.

The realization of Mullins' major goal did not occur until 1889, when legislation making attendance at post schools a military obligation for all men without an elementary education was passed.[53] By that time Mullins had stepped down as head of education in the army. His health impaired, he returned to the Twenty-fifth Infantry in the fall of 1885 and remained with the regiment for a year before poor health demanded his return home. Finally, on February 25, 1891, Chaplain George G. Mullins was retired from the army.[54]

Another chaplain, who was also to make an outstanding contribution to education in the army, reported for duty with the Twenty-fourth Infantry at Fort Supply, Indian Territory, on July 2, 1886.[55] Chaplain Allen Allensworth replaced Chaplain J. C. Laverty, who retired on February 5, 1886, after ten years' service with the regiment. Chaplain Allensworth was a black clergyman affiliated with the Baptist denomination and an ex-slave who had served in the Union Navy during the Civil War. He brought with him an excellent educational background, a degree from Roger Williams University in Nashville, Tennessee, and experience teaching in one of the schools sponsored by the Freedmen's Bureau.[56]

Allensworth's application for the position of regimental chaplain of the Twenty-fourth Infantry had to pass several political hurdles to be accepted. He knew his confirmation by the Senate would not be facilitated by the fact that he was a black man or that the Democratic Party was in office. Therefore, in a letter to Daniel Lamont, President Grover Cleveland's private secretary, Allensworth sought to turn the political situation to his advantage.

> A number of my Democratic friends in Kentucky and Ohio, desiring to strengthen the administration and party among my people, encouraged me to apply to the President for appointment, by him, as Chaplain in the 24th regiment of Colored Troops. . . . I assure the administration that if the appointment is made, it will not be dishonored. I want to show my people that a Democrat administration can appoint a Colored Chaplain as well as a Republican administration did, which appointed Mr. Plummer, to the 9th Calvary [sic].[57]

A number of congressmen, senators, businessmen, and clergymen, as well as Mrs. A. P. Starbird, his former owner, endorsed Allensworth's application.[58] President Cleveland made the appointment in the spring of 1886.

For his first year-and-a-half with the Twenty-fourth Infantry, Chaplain Allensworth operated the post school under the program set up by Chaplain Laverty. When the regiment was transferred to the Department of Arizona, he established his own educational program. One of his first steps was to begin training selected enlisted men to be teachers. When the War Department made elementary education compulsory for all soldiers, he was staffed and prepared for the influx of additional students. There were 118 men enrolled in his school at Fort Bayard, New Mexico, in 1889.[59] His energy, efficiency, and dedication earned Chaplain Allensworth the praise of his regimental commander.[60]

As a trained educator, Chaplain Allensworth saw the need for a graded curriculum in the post school, and he was able to devise a workable study outline for both children and enlisted men. In March 1889 he wrote a booklet, *Outline of Course of Study, and the Rules Governing Post Schools of Ft. Bayard, N.M.*, which detailed the graded levels of his program and reviewed the content of each subject taught at every level. He separated his program into two parts, one for children and one for soldiers. In the program for soldiers, Allensworth designated the subject matter to be taught by the day of the week. For example, Monday was for grammar, Tuesday for arithmetic, Wednesday for bookkeeping and writing, with emphasis on military records and letters, and so on throughout the week until all the basic subjects were covered. Chaplain Allensworth's booklet reveals, in a number of ways, surprising insight concerning educational and motivational techniques useful in the classroom.[61] An advocate of visual aids, he employed commercial charts and drawings wherever possible, most of these purchased out of his own pocket.[62]

Chaplain Allensworth's achievements in ⋊ education led to an invitation to deliver a paper on the topic, "Education in the United States Army," at the annual meeting of the National Education Association in 1891. His request for official permission to attend the meeting, to be held in Toronto, Canada, was denied by the War Department on the grounds that such orders were not authorized by regulations. Only by applying for a leave of absence and paying his own expenses was Allensworth able to attend.[63]

Chaplain Allensworth, like Chaplain Mullins, viewed education in the army as a way to provide the soldier's life with a new and greater dimension and as a means for making soldiers more responsible and useful citizens. In the paper he delivered at the National Education Association meeting in Toronto he elaborated on this idea as it had been implemented by the army.

> In earlier history of the army it was considered sufficient for a soldier to be able to march and handle his gun. This view has been changed and it is now a recognized fact that to be a good soldier a man must be a good citizen, therefore the government aims at giving its soldiers a fair english [sic] education, especially a knowledge of geography and history of his country. It does this not only with a view of utilizing their increased knowledge in its defense but with a further view of returning him to civil life a more intelligent citizen and well disciplined for the business of life. To accomplish this purpose common schools are established at each garrisoned post.[64]

The educational work of the chaplains in the black infantry regiments was a vital and significant contribution to the program of education in the army. The chaplains demonstrated that a post educational program when properly conducted under enthusiastic teachers and officers had a beneficial effect on the morale, discipline, and esprit de corps of a garrison. Perhaps because their students were black men who were not far removed from the days of slavery, the chaplains could observe an excitement in the educational process that aroused in them a deeper insight into the transforming qualities of education. Significantly, it was this kind of insight that enabled Chaplain Mullins to give direction and purpose to the total program of education in the army. During his tour of duty as Chief of Education in the army, Mullins brought into sharp focus for the War Department the important function education served in the military establishment. Many high-ranking officers became more favorably disposed toward education in the army because of Chaplain Mullins' persuasive ability to communicate its worth and value. The annual report of the Adjutant General of the army in 1882 seems to have reflected some of Mullins' ideas.

> The importance of the question of education in the army cannot be overestimated, whether we consider its immediate benefits in raising the standard of intelligence in the ranks, or its ulterior advantages to the country at large whenever the soldier re-enters civil life. After a term of salutary discipline and education, every man leaving the service becomes a factor of importance (under our system of government) in the civilization and well being of the State.[65]

The chaplains of the black infantry contributed to the formulation of a program of army education that has today developed into a vital part of military thought and planning. The position of chaplains in the black regiments was unique in the army of this period because they were assigned directly to the units with the responsibility of conducting an education program. White units might or might not have the services of a chaplain, depending on whether one was assigned to their post. Often the clergyman assigned to the fort would be a civilian who administered to the religious needs of the men on a part-time basis. The work of these regimental chaplains was far from perfect and their accomplishments in many respects were limited. Perhaps their major contribution was in helping engraft into the army the great American passion for education. An ardor for education was one of the distinctive features of the American character. To the American of the late nineteenth-century

> Education was his religion, and to it he paid the tribute both of his money and his affection; yet, as he expected his religion to be practical and pay dividends, he expected education to prepare for life—by which he meant, increasingly, jobs and professions.[66]

Chaplains Allensworth and Mullins, both committed to the moral worth of education, were in no small measure able to point to their experience with the black infantry regiments and demonstrate to the army the practical value of an educational program.

NOTES

1. General Orders Number 25, War Department, Adjutant General's Office, August 1, 1866, Twenty-fifth Infantry Regiment, Scrapbook, Commands, Mobile, RG 391, NA.

2. George R. Bentley, *A History of the Freedmen's Bureau*, p. 169. See also Dudley T. Cornish, "The Union Army as

a Training School for Negroes," *The Journal of Negro History*, XXXVII (October 1952), 368–382.

3. Ibid. See also Benjamin Quarles, *The Negro in the Civil War*, pp. 122–130, 290–296.

4. James M. McPherson, *The Negro's Civil War*, pp. 211–212.

5. Ibid., p. 211.

6. Paul H. Buck, *The Road to Reunion, 1865–1900*, pp. 166–167; Bentley, *A History of the Freedmen's Bureau*, pp. 169–171.

7. Chaplain George W. Pepper to Adjutant General, Washington, D.C., December 11, 1867, Letters Received, Adjutant General's Office, Vol. XLIII, M–Z, No. 792, 1867, RG 94, NA. See also John Eaton, *Grant, Lincoln and the Freedmen*, pp. 192–220.

8. Chaplain John N. Schultz to Adjutant General, January 2, 1869, Letters Received, Adjutant General's Office, File No. 43 S, RG 94, NA.

9. Statements of charges against Chaplain John N. Schultz, Twenty-fourth Infantry, Fort Brown, Texas, July, 1865, Selected, Appointment, Commission and Personal Branch Records (hereafter abbreviated as ACP), John N. Schultz, RG 94, NA. Chaplain Schultz was forced to resign his commission because of indiscretions with the wife of an enlisted man. The testimony in the statements of charges would indicate that at the time of the alleged indiscretion the chaplain was probably mentally disturbed.

10. Chaplain D. Elington Barr to Adjutant General, October 1, 1869, Letters Received, Adjutant General's Office, File No. 747, 1869, RG 94, NA.

11. Chaplain Barr was charged with being drunk on duty and unable to perform a funeral. The chaplain argued that he was not drunk but sick with a high fever. Colonel G. L. Andrews gave him the option to resign or to be court-martialed. After his resignation, Chaplain Barr accumulated a number of affidavits declaring that he was not drunk, including one from the post surgeon which declared that the chaplain was sick on the day in question. The War Department and President

Ulysses S. Grant refused to review his case because he had in effect removed himself from consideration by his resignation. Selected ACP, D. E. Barr, RG 94, NA.

12. Letter of appreciation from Edmund J. Davis, Governor of Texas, to Chaplain D. E. Barr, September 27, 1872, Selected ACP, D. E. Barr, RG 94, NA.

13. Report of Chaplain D. E. Barr from Fort Clark, Texas, January 2, 1871, Selected ACP, D. E. Barr, RG 94, NA.

14. Ibid., January 3, 1872, Selected ACP, D. E. Barr, RG 94, NA.

15. Post Returns, Fort Davis, Texas, April, 1875, RG 98, NA.

16. A collection of documents relating to the Chaplain George Gatewood Mullins' background and experience is in Selected ACP, G. G. Mullins, RG 94, NA.

17. Report of Chaplain G. G. Mullins from Fort Davis, Texas, July 12, 1875, Selected ACP, G. G. Mullins, RG 94, NA.

18. See report of inspection of Fort Davis, Texas, by Captain N. H. Davis, July 13, 1875, Letters Received, Inspector General's Office, File No. D113, RG 159, NA.

19. Ibid.

20. Ibid., Chaplain Mullins' report was attached to Captain Davis' report.

21. Ibid.

22. Report of Mullins from Fort Davis, Texas, November 1, 1875, Selected ACP, G. G. Mullins, RG 94, NA.

23. Bentley, *A History of the Freedmen's Bureau*, p. 170.

24. Report of Mullins from Fort Davis, Texas, March 10, 1876, Selected ACP, G. G. Mullins, RG 94, NA.

25. Ibid., July 12, 1876.

26. Ibid., August 31, 1876.

27. Ibid., October 31, 1876.

28. Ibid., January 1, 1877.

29. Ibid., May 2, 1877.

30. Ibid., October 31, 1877.

31. Ibid., August 31, 1876.

32. Ibid., February 28, 1878. Attached to this report is an extract of Order Number 148, Headquarters, Fort Davis, Texas,

September 28, 1877, which required all noncommissioned officers to attend the post school.

33. Report of Mullins from Fort Davis, Texas, December 31, 1877, Selected ACP, G. G. Mullins, RG 94, NA.

34. Mullins to Post Adjutant, December, 1878, Letters Received, Fort Davis, Texas, File No. 897, RG 98, NA.

35. A handwritten account of the military career of Mullins, Selected ACP, G. G. Mullins, RG 94, NA.

36. Mullins to Post Adjutant, December, 1878, Letters Received, Fort Davis, Texas, File No. 897, RG 98, NA.

37. Report of Mullins from Fort Davis, Texas, November 1, 1875, Selected ACP, G. G. Mullins, RG 94, NA.

38. Ibid., March 10, 1876.

39. Letter of Mullins to Adjutant General, Fort Davis, Texas, March 21, 1877, ibid.

40. Adjutant General's endorsement to Mullins' letter of March 21, 1877, ibid.

41. Copy of General Order Number 24, Headquarters of the Army, Washington, D.C., May 18, 1878, ibid.

42. Ibid.

43. U.S., Congress, House Executive Documents, *Annual Report of the Secretary of War, 1884–1885*, 48th Cong., 2d Sess., II, 878; U.S., Congress, House Executive Documents, *Annual Report of the Secretary of War, 1886–1887*, 49th Cong., 2d Sess., II, 11.

44. U.S., Congress, House Executive Documents, *Annual Report of the Secretary of War, 1881–1882*, 47th Cong., 1st Sess., II, 579–581; U.S. Congress, House Executive Documents, *Annual Report of the Secretary of War, 1882–1883*, 47th Cong., 2d Sess., II, 191–192; *Annual Report of the Secretary of War, 1884–1885*, pp. 878–879.

45. Report of Mullins from Fort Davis, Texas, September 1, 1878, Selected ACP, G. G. Mullins, RG 94, NA.

46. Mullins to Post Adjutant, December 7, 1878, Letters Received, Fort Davis, Texas, File No. 897, RG 98, NA.

47. Ibid.

48. See report of inspection of the Twenty-fifth Infantry by Lieutenant Colonel James H. Carleton, acting Assistant

Inspector General, Department of Texas, June, 1878, Letters Received, Inspector General's Office, File No. T 21, 1870, RG 159, NA.

49. Report of Mullins from Fort Davis, Texas, December 1, 1877, Selected ACP, RG 94, NA.

50. Third Endorsement by General E. O. C. Ord of report by Mullins from Fort Davis, Texas, April 1, 1879, Selected ACP, G. G. Mullins, RG 94, NA. General Ord later wrote a very complimentary endorsement for Mullins, recommending him as Chief of Education of the Army, copy in ACP of Mullins.

51. A handwritten account of the military career of Mullins, Selected ACP, G. G. Mullins, RG 94, NA.

52. Ibid.

53. U.S., Congress, House Executive Documents, *Annual Report of the Secretary of War, 1889–1890*, 51st Cong., 1st Sess., II, 62.

54. Post Returns, Fort Missoula, Montana Territory, March, 1891, RG 98, NA.

55. Post Returns, Fort Supply, Indian Territory, July, 1886, RG 98, NA.

56. A collection of documents and letters relating to Chaplain Allen Allensworth's background and experience is in Selected ACP, Allen Allensworth, RG 98, NA.

57. Allensworth to Mr. Daniel Lamont, Washington, D.C., October 6, 1885, Selected ACP, Allen Allensworth, RG 94, NA.

58. Letters recommending Allensworth for the position of Chaplain in the Twenty-fourth Infantry Regiment are in Selected ACP Allen Allensworth, RG 94, NA.

59. Report of inspection of Fort Bayard, New Mexico, March 26, 1889, Letters Received, Inspector General's Office, File No. 976, RG 159, NA.

60. Ibid.

61. A copy of Allensworth's booklet is in File No. 2884, Letters Received, Adjutant General's Office, 1889, RG 94, NA.

62. Report of inspection of Fort Bayard, New Mexico, 1890, RG 159, NA.

63. Report of Allensworth from Fort Bayard, New Mexico, November, 1891, Selected ACP, Allen Allensworth, RG 94, NA.

64. Text of Paper, "Education in the United States Army," delivered by Allensworth at the National Education Association meeting in Toronto, Canada, in 1891, ibid.

65. *Annual Report of the Secretary of War, 1882–1883*, p. 24.

66. Henry Steel Commager, *The American Mind*, p. 10.

6

The Attitude of the Army Toward the Black Infantrymen

Black soldiers had shown their effectiveness in the Civil War. After the battle of Port Hudson of 1863, *The New York Times* published the following report about the performance of black infantrymen in battle:

> I had seen these brave and hitherto despised fellows the day before, as I rode along the lines, and I had seen Gen. [Nathaniel C.] Banks acknowledge their respectful salute as he would have done that of any white troops; but still the question was—with too many—"Will they fight?" The black race was on this eventful day, to be put to the test, and the question to be settled—now and forever—whether or not they are entitled to assert their right to manhood.
>
> Nobly, indeed, they have acquitted themselves, proudly may every colored man hereafter hold up his head, and point to the record of those who fell on that bloody field.[1]

As time and events were to prove, this favorable view was not generally accepted. Although over 178,985 black men enlisted in the Union Army during the Civil War and fought in 449 engagements, of which 39 were major battles, and in spite of the fact that approximately 37,300 black soldiers died wearing Union uniforms, their military accomplishments were never fully appreciated, especially by military leaders.[2]

Fortunately, the wartime record of black soldiers in the army was not overlooked by Congress, and when that body passed the army act of July 28, 1866, it gave the black man a place in the regular army. The authorization for six black regiments in the peacetime army came from a Congress which was well disposed toward black men. In April 1866 the Thirty-ninth Congress passed the first Civil Rights Act which was meant to nullify all the implications of the Dred Scott decision. The measures which would have given federal courts jurisdiction over its provisions and the President the authority to use the armed forces in enforcement, was vetoed by President Andrew Johnson. In his veto message, Johnson expressed the view that he did not believe freed slaves merited full equality. Still on the attack, the Radicals introduced the Fourteenth Amendment, and Congress quickly passed it and sent it to the states.[3] With the Radicals thus gaining sway in Congress, it is understandable why the army legislation of 1866 included provisions for six black regiments. But still there were many army officers and politicians who doubted the usefulness of black soldiers.

From the beginning of the organization of the black regiments in 1866, there were many officers who looked upon an assignment with black troops as undesirable. So strong was the prejudice against black soldiers that some officers preferred to take a lower rank in a white regiment as an alternative to duty with a black regiment. George Armstrong Custer, when offered the rank of lieutenant colonel in a black regiment, turned it down, hoping to get an appointment in a white regiment.[4] Some officers who did serve in the black regiments later regarded it as a blot on their record and sought to avoid any references to it. General Nelson A. Miles, who from 1866 to 1869 was the regimental commander of the Fortieth Infantry Regiment, failed to mention in his memoirs that he had served in a black unit.[5] This attitude of racial prejudice was to cloud the careers of black soldiers and to deny them full recognition for their service.

As a matter of fact, the highest ranking officer in the army in the 1870s was not favorably disposed toward black soldiers. There is ample evidence that General William Tecumseh Sherman was prejudiced against blacks and had been for several years.[6] Sherman's disagreement with the South had been over the issue of secession, not slavery. His early years of military service in the South had made him sympathetic to the Southern attitude toward slavery and he remained an advocate of white supremacy even after the war.

Sherman had revealed his bias during the Civil War when he wrote Secretary of War Edwin M. Stanton about the question of the enlistment of black troops in the Union Army.

> I much prefer to keep negroes yet for some time to come in a subordinate state, for our prejudice, yours and mine, are not yet for absolute equality. . . . I would use the negroes as surplus but not spare a single white man, not one.[7]

He questioned whether the black men were capable of being competent soldiers and expressed doubts that former slaves could build bridges, roads, or conduct sorties and flank movements.[8] In a letter to his wife in 1863 he discussed his reservations about the use of black troops.

> General [Lorenzo] Thomas is here raising negro brigades. I would prefer to have this a white man's

> war and provide for the negroes after the time has
> passed. . . . With my opinions of negroes and my
> experience, yea prejudice, I cannot trust them yet.[9]

In 1866 he declared, "The white men of this country will
control it, and the negro, in mass, will occupy a subordi-
nate place as a race."[10] Eleven years later, testifying before a
congressional committee, Sherman openly stated his belief
that white soldiers were superior to black soldiers in every
way.[11]

It was his prejudice and distrust of blacks that motivated General Sherman to support a bill introduced in
1878 by Senator Ambrose E. Burnside of Rhode Island, a
wartime Union general and friend of Sherman's. The Burnside Bill, which supposedly sought to eliminate all color
distinction in the army, appeared to be progressive and to
advance black rights. In effect, the measure provided
for the removal of the word "colored" from statutes concerning the army. Senator Burnside said that his main reason for introducing the bill was to give black men the
opportunity to enlist in all regiments of the army and not
just those designated as colored regiments. In a speech on
the floor of the Senate, however, Burnside brought out
another point. He argued that the law prescribing four
black regiments was actually depriving the white men of
their rights.

> Now, the sections which I propose to repeal by this
> bill deprive white men of the right to enter the
> Ninth and Tenth Cavalry and the Twenty-Fourth
> and Twenty-Fifth Regiments of Infantry. No white
> man in the United States can enter those regiments
> as a private soldier. The law deprives him of that
> privilege.[12]

The Senator continued his argument for the bill by insisting
that he wanted to protect the rights of whites as well as

blacks to enlist in the army and be assigned to any regiment. Burnside then disclosed to the Senate that the proposed change had the approval of General Sherman. He had not only written his official endorsement, but had also related his feelings verbally to Burnside on numerous occasions. Burnside told the Senate: "He [Sherman] is in perfect accord with the bill; and although I do not have it directly from the officers in command of the departments where these regiments serve, I am satisfied from what the General of the Army has told me that they are in accord with the bill also."[13]

Some members of the Senate undoubtedly were aware that the Burnside Bill was not the simple issue it was purported to be. In fact, there were some indications that a plot was under way to eliminate black soldiers from the army. In December 1876 a letter was sent to General Benjamin F. Butler who was at that time residing in Washington, D.C. General Butler had been one of the first Union generals to enlist black troops in Union regiments during the Civil War, and after the war he had served in Congress as a representative from Massachusetts. In his political career he became a Radical Republican and an ardent supporter of black rights. The letter, addressed to General Butler, warned him of what was being proposed in respect to the black regiments in the army.

> Last session of Congress, a series of assaults was kept up by the Democrats against the colored soldiers in the regular army with the intention of disbanding the Colored Regiments. . . . A good many of the officers on recruiting service are opposed to colored troops and try all they can to keep them from enlisting, by putting them off and requiring them to bring all kind of credentials, also to read and write— which they don't require from the white recruits. They then raise the cry that the Colored Regiments cant get recruits. They tried the same thing 6 years

ago when Genl Grant ordered them to open recruiting offices in the South and in three months all the
Colored Regiments were full and recruiting was
then stopped for Colored troops for nearly five
years until the Colored Regiments were depleted by
discharges when they raised the cry of cant get
colored recruits. Some of the members also got up
bogus returns as to the relative cost of white and
Colored Cavalry among them taking the year when
the Colored Cavalry Regiments were remounted and
bringing up two white Cav. Regiments who had
been remounted the year before. Then saying that
in such a year two white Cav. Regiments killed no
horses, while the Colored lost so many.

General you are too well aware of the way that
the haters of the negro put their falsehoods before
the public as true. They also claim that they have a
desire to enlist both white and colored men in the
same Regiment. Neither the white nor the Colored
Soldiers desire such a thing. As soon as the Colored
are done away with they will refuse to enlist any
more colored men and so there is no way for a
colored man to compel a recruiting officer to take
him, the colored soldier would soon be a thing of
the past. . . . A good many of the Officers of
Colored Regiments are in favor of mixing the soldiers simply because they are ashamed of being in a
Colored Regiment and fancy that they are looked
down upon.[14]

This letter was signed by E. K. Davies of Brownsville,
Texas; a signature which, due to an ironic error, was to gain
more attention than it would have normally. The manner in
which Davies signed his name made it appear at a glance as
Davis rather than Davies. General Butler obviously mistook
the signature of E. K. Davies for that of E. J. Davis, the
Radical Republican governor of Texas from 1870 to 1874,
and before that, the most important Texan to fight in the

Union Army during the Civil War, having served under the command of General Butler.[15] Governor Davis' support and sympathy for blacks was well known to General Butler. In a disputed Texas election of 1874, Governor Davis had relied upon a black militia unit to assist him in attempting to keep the newly elected Democratic administration out of the statehouse.[16] Consequently, General Butler, obviously thinking the letter was from the former governor, accredited the opinions expressed in it, sent it to the Secretary of War, and added some praise for the record Davis had compiled as governor of Texas.

The Secretary of War, on the basis of General Butler's comments, sent the letter to General of the Army William T. Sherman for his remarks. Sherman called the Davies letter a "libel on the army" and added the insinuation that black men did not make good soldiers.

> The Blacks are a quiet, kindly, peaceful race of men. Naturally not addicted to war; better suited to the arts of peace. The experiment of converting them into soldiers has been honorably, and in good faith, tried in the Army of the United States, and has been partially successful; but the army is not and should not be construed a charitable institution. Congress limits its numbers for financial reasons, and we must get along with a minimum number, which should be the *best*.
>
> I advise that the word black be obliterated from the Statute Book; that whites and blacks be enlisted and distributed alike, as has been the usage in the Navy for a hundred years.[17]

Knowledge of Sherman's attitude toward the black man makes it difficult to assume that the general sincerely believed that they would be recruited among the various regiments on an equal basis. The final touch of irony in the matter of the Davies letter is disclosed by a close examination of the concluding sentence which reveals that Davies himself was a black man.[18]

At the time the Davies letter was being read at the War Department, General E. O. C. Ord was writing a letter to his friend Lieutenant Colonel William R. Shafter of the Twenty-fourth Infantry stationed at Fort Duncan, Texas. Ord was the commanding general of the Department of Texas where three of the four black regiments were stationed. In his letter General Ord stated his belief that the Burnside Bill would pass when brought to the floor of Congress, and he confided that he had supported the movement to eliminate all black units by giving testimony which implied that black companies required twice as many officers as did white companies of equal size. The reasons the additional officers were needed, Ord said, was because of the general ignorance of the black soldiers, the lack of intelligent noncommissioned officers, and the character of blacks as a race. Ord expressed confidence that his testimony would aid in the passage of the Burnside Bill.[19] When the bill was not brought to the floor of the Senate in that session of Congress, Ord wrote Shafter again, saying that he hoped the bill would be introduced in the next session. He told Shafter that he was continuing to do what he could in support of the measure.

> I am now using my best efforts to get all the regiments in the army placed on the same footing and to have no change but that, and an increase in rank and file made by the coming Congress and think the change will be made. . . . As soon as you get white troops I think all the officers of the colored regiment will feel animated with the sentiment that their work will be appreciated and do their best.[20]

The Burnside Bill was brought to the floor of the Senate for debate on April 2, 1878. In addition to his plea for the right of both whites and blacks to enlist in any

regiment, Senator Burnside called attention to the difficulty
of recruiting black soldiers. This was one of the arguments
that the Davies letter had warned would be used. Senator
Samuel D. Maxey of Texas expressed some reservations
about the prospects of mixing white and black soldiers in
the same tents and of the two races eating at the same
messes. However, he saw another possibility in the Burnside
Bill and admitted as much.

> MR. INGALLS [Kansas]. Does not the Senator from
> Texas think that if this bill became law it would re-
> sult in the absolute exclusion of all colored soldiers
> from the Army?
> MR. MAXEY. That has been a very grave question to
> my mind as to what would be the effect. As I stated
> before, I am in favor of taking the very best recruits
> that can be obtained for the service; I believe the
> white troops to be the best; and if I were a recruit-
> ing officer I would without hesitation, not regarding
> it as a question of color at all but regarding it as a
> question of duty, select white troops because I be-
> lieve them to be the best. If that construction were
> placed upon the law by the recruiting officers, my
> judgment is if the Senator desires my judgment
> about it, that you would have the Ninth and Tenth
> Regiments of cavalry and the Twenty-fourth and
> Twenty-fifth Regiments of infantry better than they
> are now. . . . If I believed it would result in convert-
> ing these two regiments of cavalry and two of in-
> fantry into good white regiments, the service would
> be bettered.[21]

Senator Maxey's remarks opened the debate on the real
issue involved in the bill. Immediately, Senator Allison of
Iowa pointed out the ambiguity of the wording in the bill
and suggested that it could be interpreted as meaning the
exclusion of all black troops from the army: "If I under-

stood the Senator from Texas, his object is to break up practically the four colored regiments that are now in the Army and to substitute in the place of those colored men, white troops."[22] Amendments were then offered to change the wording so that the bill could not be construed as Senator Maxey had implied it would be. Senator Burnside, seeing the mood of the Senate, asked to have the bill referred back to the Military Affairs Committee. His request was honored by the Senate.

The bill was brought back to the floor of the Senate for reconsideration on April 8, 1878. In the debate that ensued Senator Thomas Bayard of Delaware questioned Senator Burnside on his contention that the rights of white men were being abused by the requirement for four all-black regiments.

> MR. BAYARD. May I ask the honorable Senator whether any white men have made complaint that they were not allowed to enlist in the colored regiments?
>
> MR. BURNSIDE. I do complain myself.
>
> MR. BAYARD. Have they complained?
>
> MR. BURNSIDE. The law is distinct that these regiments shall be composed of colored men.
>
> MR. BAYARD. Has there been any complaint that that privilege has not been allowed to white men?
>
> MR. BURNSIDE. I complain myself that they are not allowed to enlist in these regiments, and my complaint is that the regiments are less efficient for the reason that white men are not allowed to enlist in them. The General of the Army complains of it; the generals in command of departments complain of it.

At this point in the exchange Senator John Ingalls of Kansas struck at the heart of the motivations behind the bill.

MR. INGALLS. The Senator from Rhode Island said a moment ago that the General of the Army was in complete accord with the purposes of this bill.

MR. BURNSIDE. Yes, sir.

MR. INGALLS. From which I judge that he is acquainted with his sentiments upon the question of the enlistment of Africans in the Army. Will the Senator inform the Senate whether the General of the Army favors the enlistment or the exclusion of persons of African descent from the regular Army?

MR. BURNSIDE. Yes, sir; I will with great pleasure.

MR. INGALLS. The reason why I ask the question is this: whatever may be the objects of this bill, I have no doubt that the results of it will be if it is passed into a law, that within five years there will not be a colored man in the United States Army.

MR. [JAMES G.] BLAINE. Within two years.

MR. INGALLS. The Senator from Maine says "two years." I accept the amendment. As the law and Constitution now stand, there is an absolute right on the part of colored as well as white men to enlist in the Army; but, as was developed in the debate the other day, there is, from some cause or other, a prejudice on the part of the officers of the Army, those who have charge of the recruiting service, so that colored men are excluded when they offer themselves; and now, if you abolish and abrogate this portion of the law that sets apart four regiments where they can be received, the result will be that this prejudice, this hostility to the enlistment of colored men, will be so great that they will have no place whatever in this branch of the public service. That I believe will be the actual result of this bill, whatever may be its purposes and its objects.

MR. BURNSIDE. Well—[23]

The intent of the Burnside Bill was obvious to all. The Senate presumedly believed it was better to have the regiments segregated than to deny black men the opportunity to serve in the army. Senator George Edmunds of Vermont provided a fitting conclusion to the debate on the bill, when he declared:

> I am satisfied from the course of things that it [the Burnside Bill] is equivalent to disbanding those regiments as colored regiments, entirely, and to the practical exclusion of the colored man, a citizen of the United States, from enlistment and promotion and appointment in the Army . . . it is no reproach to this race, nothing against them, that the [current] statute undertakes to protect them while protection is necessary in doing their share to maintain the honor and credit of the United States in the Army, and thus I think it is much better to leave the law as it stands for the time being.[24]

The Senate decided to postpone a vote on the measure indefinitely and Senator Burnside did not press the issue again.

In 1877, additional evidence that some high-ranking officers wanted the black regiments removed from the army was revealed in testimony before the House Military Affairs Committee concerning Texas border troubles. The subject of black troops was brought up in the hearings because three black regiments were stationed in Texas at the time. Lieutenant General Philip H. Sheridan, commander of the Military Division of the Missouri, testified before the committee that he believed it would be best for the service "to do away with the law which specified colored regiments, and let them [blacks and whites] be merged together."[25] General E. O. C. Ord repeated his belief that black companies required at least twice the number of officers as white companies. He also declared that the best black men did not enlist but only the drifters or those forced to enlist to avoid trouble with the law.[26] Lieutenant Colonel John Mason, Inspector General for the Department of

Texas, offered the opinion that the black troops should be removed and replaced with white soldiers because of the blacks' inefficiency.[27] Colonel H. B. Clitz of the Tenth Infantry, stationed at Fort MacKavitt, Texas, told the committee that the black infantry cost about one-fifth more than white infantry. The reason for the increased cost, he stated, was because "the Negroes are not self-sustaining; they have no mechanics, no clerks, very few of them know how to read and write; . . . they lose many more equipments [*sic*] than the whites do. . . ."[28] It was apparent from the testimony of these senior officers that they wanted to discredit black soldiers and hoped to persuade the committee to recommend enactment of legislation that would break up the black regiments.

Was there, in fact, as these officers claimed, a serious argument for removing the black regiments because of inefficiency? Were black soldiers unadaptable to army life? The answers to these questions are perhaps best found by examining regimental records, official correspondence, and reports of inspections; also the statements of officers assigned to the black infantry should be included, for they, serving with the black soldiers on a day-to-day basis were in the best position to know how they actually performed.

The soldierly qualities of the black infantryman were recorded early in their career in Texas. On June 14, 1870, Lieutenant Colonel James H. Carleton inspected the Twenty-fifth Infantry at San Antonio, Texas, and in his report spoke of the high quality of military bearing evidenced by the regiment, particularly the military appearance of the noncommissioned officers and the band. His overall impression of the regiment was good, and he was especially complimentary of the officers and their attention to duties.[29] Captain James Curtis, acting Inspector General for the Department of Texas, inspected units of the Twenty-fourth Infantry in April 1870, and his report was as favorable to the black infantry as that of Colonel Carleton.[30]

All the inspection reports submitted from the Inspector General of the Department of Texas during the early 1870s indicated that the companies of the black infantry maintained good military discipline and appearance. Not only was their desertion rate consistently among the lowest in the army, but the morale and esprit de corps of the regiments were observed to be high in spite of the isolated location of their posts.[31] In contradiction to other testimony before the House Military Affairs Committee, Lieutenant Colonel John Mason of the Department of Texas told the group that he believed the black infantry did not cost any more to equip and maintain than did white infantry. In fact, he was complimentary of the manner in which the black infantry took care of its equipment.[32] Contrary to the information furnished to Senator Burnside by General Sherman, there was evidence that enlistments in the black infantry could maintain the companies at authorized strength when efforts were made by the recruiting officers to recruit black soldiers. As a matter of fact, one officer in the Twenty-fourth Infantry in 1873 complained that officers of the black regiments had little opportunity to go on recruiting service because their units were always at full strength owing to re-enlistments and new recruits sent from the general recruiting service.[33] It would seem that if there were problems in recruiting it was not due to the unwillingness of black men to serve in the army.

In April 1877 several company officers from the black infantry gave supportive testimony before the House Military Affairs Committee on behalf of their troops. It should be noted that these officers had nothing to gain by deliberately exaggerating the capabilities of the black soldiers. Should the black regiments be disbanded, only the enlisted men would be replaced, not the officers, who would then be in command of white troops and relieved of the stigma of serving in a black unit. Captain J. W. Clous of the Twenty-fourth Infantry stated that he considered the black soldier to be as good as any other soldier in the army.[34] Captain Lewis Johnson of the Twenty-fourth told the Congressmen that he was convinced the black infantry regiments were as good and as efficient as any white regiment, and he called their attention to the fact that black soldiers did not desert as frequently as did white soldiers.[35] These opinions were not uncommon among officers serving in the black infantry regiments at that time.

Correspondence from the regiments discloses that the officers of the black infantry companies were sensitive to any criticism of their men. Captain Charles Bentzoni of the Twenty-fifth Infantry was a good example of those officers who took pride in their men and their soldierly attributes. The inspection reports invariably commented on the high degree of military bearing and efficiency displayed by Bentzoni's company. Like many other officers of the black infantry, Captain Bentzoni had served in a black infantry regiment during the Civil War and, as a result, had a sincere appreciation of the abilities and qualities of the black soldiers.[36]

In November 1875 the Chief Quartermaster of the Department of Texas issued a circular letter pertaining to the delivery of mail. According to the circular, many posts would be required to furnish mail riders from among their own men. The Quartermaster went on to say that because all the posts between Fort Concho and El Paso were garrisoned by black companies, and since black troops as a rule were not reliable, other arrangements would be made. However, prior to the issuance of the Quartermaster's circular letter, Captain Bentzoni had received orders detailing his men to provide mail service between Fort Davis and Fort Quitman. Mail delivery had begun on October 11 and as of November 7 the men of Bentzoni's command had traveled over 2,140 miles on this detail. Consequently, Bent-zoni was offended by the remarks of the Quartermaster, whom he answered by writing to the Postmaster General through the headquarters of the Department of Texas.

> In justice to the troops which I have the honor to command, I take this opportunity to state. . . . That it [the mail] has arrived and departed punctually and has been delivered in good order. . . . No civilians have been employed in carrying the mail, the soldiers being considered competent and reliable to perform this as well as any other ordinary duty which may be required of them.[37]

Colonel George L. Andrews, the commanding officer of the Twenty-fifth Infantry, was particularly sensitive to any evidence of prejudice against the black soldiers. In official relationships with his men, he attempted to be fair and honest and was respected by the officers and enlisted men of his regiment.[38] Typical of his concern that his men be accorded fair treatment was an incident concerning an inspection at Fort Randall, Dakota Territory. Andrews was absent from the post in November 1881 when the inspection was made. Later, in a letter to the Assistant Adjutant General of the department, he drew attention to the fact that his officers believed the inspecting officer was "strongly prejudiced" against black soldiers.[39] A short time later a reply was received from General A. H. Terry, the department commander, enclosing a statement from Major W. W. Sanders, the inspecting officer, in which the latter denied any prejudice against black troops. The general also assured Colonel Andrews that Major Sanders was not anti-black, that he had even served with the black troops of another regiment, and that he had probably been misunderstood when comparing them to the men of the Twenty-fifth.[40]

Colonel Z. R. Bliss, regimental commander of the

Twenty-fourth Infantry, exhibited concern for fair treatment when in August 1886 a black recruit was sent to Fort Supply, Indian Territory, from Fort Leavenworth, Kansas, with only a day's rations. Because of a clerk's error regarding transportation schedules, the recruit had been required to spend the weekend in Kiowa, Kansas, since no stagecoach was leaving for Fort Supply until Monday. As a result, when the soldier reported at Fort Supply, he had been without rations for four days. Colonel Bliss called attention to the incident in a letter to the Assistant Adjutant General of the Department of Missouri.[41] Although his letter was in the form of a request for commutation for rations, he was obviously also letting the department headquarters know that one of his men had been improperly treated.

This kind of sensitivity and concern often resulted in a close relationship between officers and men in the black regiments. Frederic Remington, the western artist, noted this closeness while accompanying a patrol from a black unit.

> Personal relations can be much closer between white officers and colored soldiers than in white regiments without breaking the barriers which are necessary to army discipline. The men look up to a good officer, rely on him in trouble, and even seek him for advice in their small personal affairs.[42]

The officers sometimes went out of their way to assist their men when they needed special help. On one occasion, Colonel Andrews requested that a private in his regiment whom he considered an excellent soldier, be given special medical attention at a government hospital so that he might return to duty rather than be discharged.[43] A commanding officer would make such a request only because he was concerned for the welfare of the particular individual.

The close relationship between officers and men was undoubtedly a factor in the outstanding record the black infantry regiments continued to uphold during their service on the frontier in the 1880s. The inspecting officer at Fort Hale, in 1883, was appalled at the wretched conditions under which the officers and men of the Twenty-fifth were compelled to live. Yet he was amazed at their military bearing: "I am disposed to think that all things considered, Captain Schooley's company presented the best general appearance of all the companies in the Department of Dakota I have inspected."[44] In Indian Territory, in 1887, an inspector of a battalion of the Twenty-fourth reported that both officers and noncommissioned officers of the infantry were proficient men. He was particularly impressed with the performance of the enlisted men and the above-average neatness of their barracks.[45] Similarly, a colonel of the First Cavalry Regiment wrote to Captain Owen J. Sweet, the commanding officer of Company D of the Twenty-fifth:

> In making the Bi-monthly inspection of this post [Fort Custer] for October, 1889, I am pleased to inform you that I found your Company "D", 25th Inf. and Barracks it occupies not only clean and in satisfactory condition, in all respects, but I think the Company and Barracks were the cleanest I ever inspected since being in the service.[46]

The field and tactical training ratings of the black infantry regiments were as good as those on their garrison performance.[47] Then men of the Twenty-fourth and Twenty-fifth Infantry were by any standard competent soldiers.

In short, the army attitude toward the black infantry regiments appears to have been conditioned either by experience or prejudice. Those who had served with black troops were usually satisfied with their ability as soldiers;

those who lacked firsthand experience with black troops appeared to be guided more by their prejudices. For instance, General A. H. Terry, the commanding officer of the Department of Dakota, defended black soldiers on the basis of his experiences with them. In 1885 a citizen of Sturgis City, Dakota Territory wrote President Grover Cleveland asking for the removal of the black troops. Asked to comment on the letter, General Terry wrote:

> I have had much experience with colored troops, and I have always found them well behaved, and as amenable to discipline, as any white troops we have; the characteristic submissiveness of their race is manifested in the readiness with which they yield to military control.
>
> They are much more temperate than our white troops, and crime and disorders resulting from intoxication are comparatively rare among them.[48]

On the other hand, General Sherman had not had direct experience with black troops.[49] It is apparent that Sherman's own bias and lack of concrete experience with black soldiers distorted his judgment as to their value. As late as 1880, General Sherman was still advocating the removal of the black regiments. In his annual report of that year he argued that the law requiring separate black units was not consistent with the Fourteenth Amendment and should be removed from the statute books.[50] It was the same line of reasoning that had been used by Senator Ambrose E. Burnside in 1878.

Army prejudice against black soldiers appeared under different guises. There were instances of officers attempting to make the duty of the black soldiers as unpleasant as possible, but most often prejudice took the form of paternalism.[51] Racial bias also appeared in the official records of various units and departments of the army, as it was commonly believed that black people were not only physically different from whites, but naturally immune to tropical diseases and able to withstand tropical climates better than whites.[52] This belief was given credence by the Surgeon General who maintained two sets of medical statistics, one for white and one for black troops. General Sherman also subscribed to this view and stated it before the House Military Affairs Committee in 1877.

> The special reason, however, for keeping them [the black regiments] on the Texas frontier is what I have already stated, their supposed better adaptation to that climate. They are less liable to typhoid fevers than white troops, and really we have had some very painful instances of the effects of typhoid fever upon white troops down there. The black troops are better able to stand that climate than white troops, especially in the summer months.[53]

It was solely due to the constant complaints of the white officers that the black infantry regiments were finally transferred after ten years of hard duty on the Texas border.

The logical extension of this racial myth was that the black troops could be expected to experience suffering and sickness if sent to the Northern climates. When the Twenty-fifth Infantry was transferred to Dakota Territory, the Surgeon General took the opportunity to observe the effects of the cold weather upon black troops. In his annual report of 1887, the Surgeon General revealed the findings in his study: "It appears that the non-effective rate of the colored troops in the northern group was about the same as that of the white."[54] If this evidence subverted the racial myth concerning blacks in colder climates, another report was doing equal damage to their reputed immunity to malarial diseases in southerly climates.

Malarial fevers were the principal cause of admission among the colored troops, their rate for this class of disease being 383.78, considerably in excess of that of the white troops, which was 210.71 per 1000 of mean strength.[55]

Nor were all the officers who served with black troops immune to racial prejudice. Complaints by the men of the black infantry regiments that certain officers mistreated them did occur, and it is difficult to determine by the evidence available whether actual mistreatment existed in each case. One example was an anonymous letter sent to the Secretary of War in 1888 alleging that the officers at Fort Shaw, Montana Territory, were prejudiced against black soldiers. The anonymous letter, written a few days after the lynching of Private Robert Robinson, stated that the commanding officer, Lieutenant Colonel J. J. VanHorn, had released Private Robinson to civilian authorities knowing there was a good chance he would be lynched.[56] The unknown author also stated that the commanding officer had openly declared his dislike for blacks and treated them as if they were still slaves.[57] Whether this complaint was based on fact or frustration over the event to which it was related cannot be determined. But at least one officer at Fort Shaw who was directly involved in turning Private Robinson over to civil authorities did at a later time exhibit a condescending atttitude toward blacks. While on bivouac with the Twenty-fifth Infantry near Fort Keogh, Montana, during the Pine Ridge Campaign, Lieutenant G. P. Ahren wrote a local newspaper:

We have a strong force of infantry and cavalry here on the northwest corner of the war. Our "cullud" battalion here is under canvas and in fine shape for a winter campaign, and when Jack Frost freezes the mercury out of sight the gay and festive coon will be found ready to dance the "Virginia essence" and sing as joyfully as ever.[58]

By the late 1870s, the army, like the civilian society it mirrored, was becoming less concerned for the welfare of the black man than it had been earlier. With President Rutherford B. Hayes' election and the withdrawal of the army from the South, solicitude for these newly enfranchised citizens began to decrease. After 1877, northerners were for the most part in substantial agreement with southerners in believing that blacks were not prepared for equality and, as a race, inferior to whites.[59] This kind of thinking was displayed in the remarks of General J. M. Schofield, Superintendent of the Military Academy at West Point, in his annual report of 1880. The academy had been the object of an investigation following charges of racial discrimination against black cadets.

> The prevailing "prejudice" is rather a just aversion to qualities which the people of the United States have long been accustomed to associate with a state of slavery and intercourse without legal marriage, and of which color and its various shades are only the external signs. That feeling could not be removed by the simple act of enfranchising the slave. It can only be done by the education and moral elevation of the race. That great work has only commenced, and it must of necessity require much time. To send to West Point for four years' competition a young man who was born in slavery is to assume that half a generation has been sufficient to raise a colored man to the social, moral, and intellectual level which the average white man has reached in several hundred years. As well might the common farm horse be entered in a four mile race against the best blood inherited from a long line of English racers.[60]

Prevalent among many army officers was the belief that blacks should be accorded fair treatment so long as it did not involve social or intellectual equality.

That black men were aware of this growing attitude of paternalism is evidenced in the correspondence of Chaplain Allen Allensworth, a black man. Since army chaplains were nominated by the President, Allensworth recognized the need for Senate support for his nomination. In a letter to Senator J. E. Brown of Georgia, his awareness of the current white attiudes is apparent:

> I will respectfully state, that I am and have been on pleasant terms with the Whites of my state, and my relations with them pleasant, and that in all my relations with them, I have never given them occasion to complain of any attempt of mine to intrude upon their social convictions or usages. Their opinions in such matters I respect and have respected. Allow me to further say: that my Southern training has taught me enough to know how to appreciate the position of those, who are my superiors, intellectually, socially, and financially, and to act according to my relation to them, without undue assumption.[61]

Chaplain Allensworth was even more explicit in a letter to the Adjutant General of the army. Shortly after he had applied for the position he was informed that his application would not receive favorable consideration due to the fact that Chaplains received officer status and, since he was black, this would cause social problems. Anticipating these objections, Allensworth made it clear that he knew his "position."

> I know where the official ends and where the Social life begins and have therefore guraded [*sic*] against Social intrusion. . . . I know to some extent, what the feelings of the officers in the Army and Navy are on this subject, and am prepared to guard against allowing myself in any position to give offense.[62]

With Allensworth's appointment to regimental chaplain, there were only two black commissioned officers in the army—both of them chaplains. Perhaps they were accepted because chaplains were never allowed command positions and remained at the equivalent rank of captain throughout their army careers.

It was in this climate of opinion that the black infantry regiments served in the army. Contrary to the attention accorded their white counterparts, black infantrymen received little, if any, recognition for their years of frontier service—another of the many injustices done to blacks in America. Even when by the army's own criteria they proved themselves to be superior units, the shadow of racial prejudice kept them from receiving their due. Despite the black soldiers having the best record in the service regarding desertion and alcoholism, the army's two major problems during the 1870s and 1880s, they received but casual acknowledgment for their outstanding records.

In 1889 Secretary of War Redfield Proctor did mention that the rate of desertions in the black regiments was only two percent compared to twelve percent for white regiments.[63] That same year General J. C. Kelton, the Adjutant General, suggested that the major cause of desertion was administrative.

> This is obvious to anyone who . . . critically examines the statistics presented. He will soon discover . . . that a discipline of a kind in which the interests of the soldier are little considered . . . and desertion go together. The ideal steadfast soldier in a volunteer army such as the regular army is . . . can only be secured by equitable and considerate treatment combined with the exactions of military duty.[64]

By the Adjutant General's own standards it would appear that the officers of the black infantry regiments were "equitable and considerate" in dealing with their men.

The absence in the black regiments of excessive drinking and alcoholism[65]—two major army problems—was reported by the Surgeon General in his annual report of 1889.

> The difference between the rate of white and colored troops in this case [alcoholism] is most noteworthy: admissions, whites 43.97; colored 4.55; non-effectiveness, white, .44, colored, .03. This should be printed in italic to the credit of the colored soldiers.[66]

Official army studies of chronic alcoholism did not indicate a correlation between drinking and the isolation of frontier duty. Perhaps it can be reasoned that the rate of alcoholism was dependent upon morale rather than on location.[67] If this was the case, it could be argued that among the regiments of the army, the black soldiers had the best morale.

This evidence was not entirely overlooked by the army. The Secretary of War in his recommendations to the President in 1889 suggested, without success, that the two additional regiments of artillery sought by the army should be composed of black soldiers. In his remarks the Secretary of War gave the black infantry regiments one of their rare compliments from the higher levels of army administration. Commenting on their excellent record of service, he pointed out that they were "neat, orderly, and obedient, are seldom brought before courts martial and rarely desert."[68] Also, some frontier commanders were aware that the Twenty-fourth and Twenty-fifth infantries were first-class regiments. General Nelson A. Miles evidently thought so when, in 1886, he reported that the Apaches in Arizona were getting out of hand and requested that either the Twenty-fourth or Twenty-fifth infantries be sent to replace the First Infantry.[69] Miles, having previously served with black troops, was undoubtedly aware of their fine record and military abilities. Had he considered them to be substandard regiments, he would hardly have made the request.

The army's official response to black soldiers was to an extent conditioned by the racial attitudes current in American society of that period. By the end of the 1880s and the beginning of the 1890s the civil rights of black citizens were being circumvented by legal and legislative machinations at state and federal levels.[70] Apart from that, the army attitude toward the black infantry regiments appears to have been based either on direct personal experience with black troops or personal racial prejudice. The evidence seems clear that those officers and commanders who had personal experience or had served with black troops were usually satisfied with their ability as soldiers. Conversely, it appears that those who did not have firsthand experience with black troops were guided more by their prejudice. Both types of response are reflected in official army correspondence. Personal involvement with black troops promoted understanding and served to destroy racial stereotypes. Noninvolvement however, permitted official opinion to follow stereotyped notions and the prejudices common at that time. Yet, in spite of its obvious prejudices and shortcomings, the army gave the black man a measure of human dignity and worth that few institutions in American society of that period could offer.

NOTES

1. *New York Times*, June 13, 1863.
2. James M. McPherson, *The Negro's Civil War*, p. 237.
3. Eric L. McKitrick, *Andrew Johnson and Reconstruction*, pp. 12–13; J. G. Randall and David Donald, *The Civil War and Reconstruction*, pp. 568–569.

4. William H. Leckie, *The Buffalo Soldiers*, p. 8.

5. Nelson A. Miles, *Personal Recollections of General Nelson A. Miles*, p. 51.

6. John G. Barrett, *Sherman's March Through the Carolinas*, pp. 4, 8, 30, 31 245, 278; B. H. Liddell Hart, *Sherman, Soldier, Realist, American*, pp. 198, 352–353; M. A. DeWolfe Howe, ed., *Home Letters of General Sherman*, pp. 178–179, 229, 252–253, 353; Robert K. Murray, "General Sherman, the Negro, and Slavery," *The Negro History Bulletin*, XII (March, 1959) 125–130; Rachel Sherman Thorndike, ed., *The Sherman Letters.*, pp. 248, 252, 262–263.

7. Quoted in Benjamin P. Thomas and Harold M. Hyman, *Stanton*, p. 343. See also Barrett, *Sherman's March Through the Carolinas*, p. 31, for a confirmation of this attitude.

8. Barrett, *Sherman's March*, p. 30.

9. General Sherman from Camp opposite Vicksburg, to Mrs. Sherman, April 17, 1863, in Howe, ed., *Letters of Sherman*, pp. 252–253.

10. General Sherman to Senator John Sherman, Headquarters, Military Division of the Mississippi, St. Louis, Missouri, February 23, 1866, in Thorndike, ed., *The Sherman Letters*, p. 263.

11. U.S., Congress, House, Committee on Military Affairs, House Miscellaneous Documents, No. 64, *Testimony on the Texas Border Troubles*, 45th Cong., 2d Sess., 1877, VI, 20.

12. U.S., Congress, Senate, 45th Cong., 2d Sess., April 18, 1878, *Congressional Record, 2325.*

13. Ibid.

14. E. K. Davies to General B. F. Butler, December 7, 1876, Letters Received, Adjutant General's Office, File No. 510, 1877, RG 94, NA.

15. Frank H. Smyrl, "Texans in the Union Army," *Southwestern Historical Quarterly*, LXV (October 1961), 234–250.

16. Otis A. Singletary, "The Texas Militia During Reconstruction," *Southwestern Historical Quarterly*, LX (July 1956), 33.

17. Sherman's endorsement on E. K. Davies' letter, January 30, 1877. Letters Received, Adjutant General's Office, File No. 510, RG 94, NA.

18. The last sentence of the Davies letter reads: "I respect-fully on behalf of the Colored men in the Regular Army adress [*sic*] you this letter, hoping that you will be pleased to give it that consideration which you always do to anything pertaining to our race." E. K. Davies to General B. F. Butler, December 7, 1876, Letters Received, Adjutant General's Office. File No. 510, 1877, RG 94, NA.

19. Letter of General E. O. C. Ord to Lieutenant Colonel W. R. Shafter, January 3, 1877, Stanford University Library, William R. Shafter Papers.

20. Ibid., October 3, 1877.

21. U.S., Congress, Senate, 45th Cong., 2d Sess., April 2, 1878, *Congressional Record*, 2190.

22. Ibid., 2191.

23. Ibid., April 8, 1878, 2325–2326.

24. Ibid., April 17, 1878, 2602.

25. U.S., Congress, House, Committee on Military Affairs, House Miscellaneous Documents, No. 64, *Testimony on the Texas Border Troubles,* 45th Cong., 2d Sess., 1877, VI, 70.

26. Ibid., 103.

27. Ibid., 125.

28. Ibid., 125.

29. Report of inspection of the Twenty-fifth Infantry at San Antonio, Texas, by Lieutenant Colonel James H. Carleton, June 20, 1870, Letters Received, Inspector General's Office, File No. T 21, RG 159, NA.

30. Report of inspection of the Twenty-fourth Infantry at Fort Richardson, Texas, by Captain James Curtis, April 5, 1870; Report of inspection of the Twenty-fourth Infantry at Fort Concho, Texas, by Captain James Curtis, April 17, 1870, both in Letters Received, Inspector General's Office, File No. T 14, RG 159, NA.

31. Report of inspection of Fort Davis, Texas, by Captain N. H. Davis, n.d., Letters Received, Inspector General's Office, File No. D 113, 1875, RG 159, NA.

32. U.S., Congress, House, Committee on Military Affairs, House Miscellaneous Documents, No. 64, *Testimony on the Texas Border Troubles,* 45th Cong., 2d Sess., 1877, VI, 120–121.

33. Captain H. C. Corbin to General of the Army, Decem-

ber 4, 1873, Letters Received, Headquarters, United States Army, XCIV, 68, RG 94, NA.

34. U.S., Congress, House, Committee on Military Affairs, House Miscellaneous Documents, No. 64, *Testimony on the Texas Border Troubles*, 45th Cong., 2d Sess., 1877, VI, 130.

35. Ibid., 142.

36. William H. Powell, *List of Officers of the Army of the United States from 1779 to 1900*, p. 192.

37. Captain Charles Bentzoni to the Postmaster General, through the Commanding Officer, Department of Texas, November 27, 1875, Letters Sent, Fort Quitman, Texas, File No. 75, RG 393, NA.

38. The official correspondence of Colonel G. L. Andrews shows his fairness in all matters dealing with his officers and men. A search of the records of the Twenty-fifth Infantry did not disclose any significant evidence to indicate there were complaints against Colonel Andrews for any reason.

39. Colonel G. L. Andrews to Assistant Adjutant General, Department of Dakota, January 4, 1882, Letters Sent, Fort Randall, Dakota Territory, RG 393, NA.

40. General A. H. Terry to Colonel G. L. Andrews, with enclosure of statement by Major W. W. Sanders, acting Inspector General of the Department of Dakota, January 20, 1882, Letters Received, Fort Randall, Dakota Territory, File No. 50, RG 98, NA.

41. Colonel Z. R. Bliss to Assistant Adjutant General of the Department of the Missouri, August 25, 1886, Letters Sent, Fort Supply, Indian Territory, RG 393, NA.

42. Harold McCracken, ed., *Frederic Remington's Own West*, p. 69.

43. Colonel G. L. Andrews to Surgeon General, July 7, 1890, Letters Sent, Fort Missoula, Montana, RG 393, NA.

44. Captain R. P. Hughes, acting Assistant Inspector General to Adjutant General, Department of Dakota, October 12, 1883, Letters Received, Adjutant General's Office, File No. 5176, RG 94, NA.

45. Report of inspection of Fort Sill, Indian Territory, by Major G. H. Burton, October, 1887, Letters Received, Inspector General's Office, File No. 1303, RG 159, NA.

46. Colonel J. S. Brisbin to Captain O. J. Sweet, Fort Custer, Montana, November 8, 1889, Twenty-fifth Infantry Regiment, Scrapbook, Commands, Mobile, RG 391, NA.

47. See Report of inspection of Twenty-fifth Infantry Regiment at Fort Missoula, Montana, by Lieutenant Colonel W. F. Drum, Letters Received, Inspector General's Office, File No. 61, 1889; Report of inspection of Twenty-fifth Infantry Regiment at Fort Custer, Montana, by Lieutenant Colonel W. F. Drum, Letters Received, Inspector General's Office, File No. 1238, both reports in RG 159, NA.

48. General A. H. Terry to General P. H. Sheridan, November 10, 1885, Letters Received, Adjutant General's Office, File No. 6443, RG 94, NA.

49. General B. F. Butler pointed out to Secretary of War J. D. Cameron that General W. T. Sherman had not had experience with black troops. See endorsements related to the E. K. Davies letter in Letters Received, Adjutant General's Office, File No. 510, 1877, RG 94, NA.

50. U.S., Congress, House Executive Documents, *Annual Report of the Secretary of War, 1880–1881*, 46th Cong., 3d Sess., II, 6.

51. Leckie, *The Buffalo Soldiers*, pp. 13–14.

52. Kenneth M. Stampp, *The Peculiar Institution*, pp. 295–296.

53. U.S., Congress, House, Committee on Military Affairs, House Miscellaneous Documents, No. 64, *Testimony on the Texas Border Troubles*, 45th Cong., 2d Sess., 1877, VI, 20.

54. U.S., Congress, House Executive Documents, *Annual Report of the Secretary of War, 1887–1888*, 50th Cong., Ist Sess., II, 617.

55. Ibid., 618.

56. An account of this lynching is given in Chapter 3.

57. Anonymous letter from Fort Shaw, Montana Territory, to Secretary of War W. C. Endicott, July 23, 1888, Letters Received, Adjutant General's Office, File no. 3351, RG 94, NA.

58. *Stock Growers Journal* (Miles City, Montana), December 27, 1890.

59. Vincent P. De Santis, "The Republican Party Revisited, 1877–1897," in H. Wayne Morgan, ed., *The Gilded Age*, pp.

108–109; Rayford W. Logan, *The Betrayal of the Negro,* pp. 165–276; Paul H. Buck, *The Road to Reunion,* pp. 283–284.

60. *Annual Report of the Secretary of War, 1880–1881,* p. 229.

61. Allen Allensworth to Senator J. E. Brown, March 22, 1886, Selected Appointment, Commission and Personal Branch Records, Allen Allensworth, RG 94, NA.

62. Allensworth to the Adjutant General of the United States Army, March 3, 1886, ibid.

63. U.S., Congress, House Executive Documents, *Annual Report of the Secretary of War, 1889–1890,* 51st Cong., 1st Sess., II, 8.

64. Ibid., p. 84.

65. Don Rickey, Jr., *Forty Miles a Day,* p. 159.

66. *Annual Report of the Secretary of War, 1889–1890,* p. 799.

67. Rickey, *Forty Miles a Day,* pp. 159–160.

68. *Annual Report of the Secretary of War, 1889–1890,* pp. 4–5.

69. General Nelson A. Miles to the Adjutant General, May, 1886, Letters Received, Headquarters, United States Army, RG 94, NA, p. 205.

70. John Hope Franklin, *From Slavery to Freedom,* pp. 324–343; Benjamin Quarles, *The Negro in the Making of America,* pp. 126–155; C. Vann Woodward, *The Strange Career of Jim Crow,* pp. 52–56; Buck, *The Road to Reunion,* pp. 283–297.

7

Hope for a Better Day

The black community today has rightly charged that black history has been systematically ignored in the white man's history books.[1] This criticism is certainly true in the case of the Twenty-fourth and Twenty-fifth Infantry Regiments. Despite the significant role played by black infantrymen, their service on the frontier during the Indian Wars has usually been omitted from the pages of historical accounts of that period. For twenty-two years, from 1869 to 1891, from the hot, arid reaches of Texas, New Mexico, and Arizona to the frigid plains of the Dakotas and Montana, these black soldiers garrisoned forts along the frontier. Whether it was hostile Indians, bands of outlaws, or cattle thieves, the black infantry regiments successfully met their adversaries, as well as extremes of climate, in a manner that was a credit to them and the army. These rugged soldiers not only had the lowest desertion rate among all regiments in the army, but they proved to be exceptionally well-disciplined and competent troops. At a time when alcoholism was the bane of most frontier regiments, it was virtually unknown among the black units.

The story of the Twenty-fourth and Twenty-fifth infantries is unique. Many white infantry regiments performed the same duties, served at the same or similar frontier posts, but did not equal the impressive record of these black troops. The black infantry units were by any standard, first-rate regiments, a distinction they achieved in spite of their continuous assignment to isolated areas. Living in substandard quarters, often no better than mud huts, these black infantrymen consistently received excellent ratings on their military bearing and appearance. They exhibited a high esprit de corps even though they knew that because they were black men there was little chance of their being relieved from frontier duty to be stationed at posts east of the Mississippi River. This is not to suggest that all were model soldiers or that the regiments succeeded in everything they tried. There were criminals and troublemakers among their ranks, and failure was not uncommon; however, the strong allegiance to duty which characterized their service enabled them to endure the hardships of the West.

In the last analysis, racial prejudice and discrimination proved to be the two adversaries that the Twenty-fourth and Twenty-fifth infantries could not overcome. For no other reason except that their skins were black, these troops received but minimal recognition for their accomplishments. Assignments of the black infantry were dictated by a social climate of groundless prejudices.

The period following their service in the West brought no reprieve from racial prejudice and discrimination. In spite of the black infantrymen's outstanding record in the Spanish-American War, when they won the praise and respect of all who fought beside them, racial bias continued to deprive them of due recognition.[2] The Twenty-fourth and Twenty-fifth infantries are remembered more for their part in race riots than for their service on the frontier or in Cuba. In 1906, racial disorders between whites and black soldiers at Brownsville, Texas prompted President Theodore Roosevelt to discharge an entire battalion of the Twenty-fifth Infantry without honor and, further, to disqualify them from employment in either the military or civil service of the United States. This unusual punishment was later mollified by an act of Congress in 1909. Eleven years later, men of the Twenty-fourth Infantry, after being baited by whites, participated in a race riot at Houston, Texas, which resulted in the death of seventeen whites. In this instance, with only a slight pretense of a trial, thirteen black soldiers were tried and hanged, and forty others were sentenced to life imprisonment. Because of what they reasoned to be unjust treatment of their comrades, some members of the regiment vowed vengeance on the trial officials.[3] These tragic events, spawned by a segregationist society, succeeded in burying from public view the splendid record compiled by these two black regiments.

As mentioned, historians are now being challenged to state in full the black man's contribution to American life and culture. Scholarly work in the area of black military accomplishments, service, and sacrifices, can shed new light on American military history as well as on American life generally. Biographies of black officers and cadets should, for instance, raise new questions concerning the responsibility of the military establishment to the society and the form of government it seeks to defend. This study has indicated that the army, when properly motivated, can be a vehicle of significant social change. The educational program of the black infantry is a case in point. Recent history has demonstrated that the army can help in bringing about even more important social changes. It is worth noting that the United States Army saw the value of adopting a policy of integration before the Supreme Court decision of 1954.

One of the paradoxes of American history is that the traditionally conservative military establishment has led the way in providing a measure of dignity, self-respect, and hope for American minorities. Certainly for the black male of the 1870s and 1880s, the army, which was far from being a citadel of democracy and equality, did provide as fair an opportunity as the American nation could offer. And for many black citizens of that time, the black soldiers were symbols of hope for a better day. As Professor Rayford Logan of Howard University has said, "Negroes had little, at the turn of the century to help sustain our faith in ourselves except the pride that we took in the Ninth and Tenth Cavalry, the Twenty-fourth and Twenty-fifth Infantry. . . . They were our Ralph Bunche, Marian Anderson, Joe Louis, and Jackie Robinson."[4]

NOTES

1. Black scholars have called attention to this neglect of the black man's contributions to American history. See Benjamin Quarles, *The Negro in the Making of America*, pp. 7–9; and William Loren Katz, *Teachers' Guide to American Negro History*, pp. 5–8.

2. John Hope Franklin, *From Slavery to Freedom*, pp. 418–425.

3. Ibid., pp. 442–443, 460.

4. Rayford W. Logan, *The Betrayal of the Negro from Rutherford B. Hayes to Woodrow Wilson*, p. 335.

Bibliography

MANUSCRIPT MATERIALS

National Archives, Washington, D.C.
Record Group 94, Records of the War Department.
> Selected Letters Received relating to the Twenty-fourth and Twenty-fifth Infantry Regiments at Adjutant General's Office, 1866–1891.
>
> Regimental Returns of the Twenty-fourth and Twenty-fifth Infantry Regiments, 1869–1891.
>
> Selected Appointment, Commission, and Personal Branch Records for:
>> Allen Allensworth
>> D. Elington Barr
>> J. C. Laverty
>> George G. Mullins
>> John N. Schultz
>
> Letters Received, Headquarters, United States Army, 1870–1891.
>
> Letters Sent, Headquarters, United States Army, 1870–1891.

Record Group 98, Records of the War Department.
  Post Returns, 1869–1891.
    Fort Apache, Arizona Territory
    Fort Bayard, New Mexico Territory
    Fort Bliss, Texas
    Fort Brown, Texas
    Fort Clark, Texas
    Fort Concho, Texas
    Fort Davis, Texas
    Fort Duncan, Texas
    Fort Grant, Arizona Territory
    Fort Hale, Dakota Territory
    Fort Keogh, Montana Territory
    Fort McKavett, Texas
    Fort Meade, Dakota Territory
    Fort Missoula, Montana Territory
    Fort Quitman, Texas
    Fort Randall, Dakota Territory
    Fort Shaw, Montana Territory
    Fort Sill, Indian Territory
    Fort Supply, Indian Territory
  Selected Letters Received, 1870–1891:
    Fort Bayard, New Mexico Territory
    Fort Brown, Texas
    Fort Davis, Texas
    Fort Missoula, Montana Territory
    Fort Randall, Dakota Territory
    Fort Supply, Indian Territory
Record Group 159, Records of the War Department
  Reports of inspections on file in the Inspector General's
    Office, 1869–1891:
    Fort Apache, Arizona Territory
    Fort Bayard, New Mexico Territory
    Fort Concho, Texas
    Fort Custer, Montana Territory
    Fort Davis, Texas
    Fort Grant, Arizona Territory
    Fort Hale, Dakota Territory
    Fort Meade, Dakota Territory

        Fort Missoula, Montana Territory
        Fort Randall, Dakota Territory
        Fort Sill, Indian Territory
        Fort Supply, Indian Territory
        Fort Richardson, Texas
        San Antonio, Texas
Record Group 391, Records of the War Department
    Mobile Commands
        Twenty-fifth Infantry Regiment Scrapbook
Record Group 393, Records of the War Department
    Selected Letters Sent, 1869–1891:
        Fort Bayard, New Mexico Territory
        Fort Davis, Texas
        Fort Missoula, Montana Territory
        Fort Quitman, Texas
        Fort Randall, Dakota Territory
        Fort Supply, Indian Territory

MANUSCRIPT COLLECTIONS

The William Rufus Shafter Papers. Stanford University Library, Stanford, California.

UNITED STATES GOVERNMENT DOCUMENTS

Annual Report of the Secretary of War, 1866–1891.
Chronological List of Actions with Indians from January 1, 1866 to January, 1881. Office Memoranda, Adjutant General's Office, n.d., n.p., National Archives.
U.S. Congress. House. Committee on Military Affairs. House Miscellaneous Documents, Document No. 64, *Testimony on the Texas Border Troubles.* 45th Cong., 2d Sess., VI, 1877.
U.S. Congress. Senate. *Congressional Record,* 45th Cong., 2d Sess., VII, 1878.

PERIODICALS

Conway, Walter C., ed. "Colonel Edmund Shriver's Inspector General's Report on Military Posts in Texas, November, 1872—January, 1873." *Southwestern Historical Quarterly*, LXVII (April, 1964), 559–563.

Cornish, Dudley T. "The Union Army as a Training School for Negroes." *The Journal of Negro History*, XXXVII (October, 1952), 368–382.

Dalfiume, Richard M. "The 'Forgotten Years' of the Negro Revolution." *The Journal of American History*, LV (June, 1968), 90–106.

Frost, Lawrence. "Battle of the Washita." In *Great Western Indian Fights*, 1960, pp. 175–181.

Hay, Thomas R. "The South and the Arming of Slaves." *The Mississippi Valley Historical Review*, VI (June, 1919), 37–74.

McMillen, Kathryn, S. "A Descriptive Bibliography on the San Antonio-San Diego Mail Line." *Southwestern Historical Quarterly*, LIX (October, 1955), 206–214.

Murray, Robert K. "General Sherman, The Negro, and Slavery: The Story of an Unrecognized Rebel." *The Negro History Bulletin*, XXII (March, 1959), 125–130.

Porter, Kenneth W. "Negroes and Indians of the Texas Frontier." *Southwestern Historical Quarterly*, LIII (October, 1949), 151–163.

———. "The Seminole-Negro Scouts, 1870–1881." *Southwestern Historical Quarterly*, LV (January, 1952), 358–377.

Rippy, J. Fred. "Some Precedents of the Pershing Expedition into Mexico." *Southwestern Historical Quarterly*, XXIV (April, 1921), 235–292.

Singletary, Otis A. "The Texas Militia During Reconstruction." *Southwestern Historical Quarterly*, LX (July, 1956), 23–35.

Smyrl, Frank H. "Texans in the Union Army." *Southwestern Historical Quarterly*, LXV (October, 1961), 234–250.

Wallace, Edward S. "General John Lapham Bullis, Thunderbolt of the Texas Frontier, I." *Southwestern Historical Quarterly*, LIV (April, 1951), 452–461.

————. "General John Lapham Bullis, Thunderbolt of the Texas Frontier, II." *Southwestern Historical Quarterly*, LV (July, 1951), 77–85.

————. "General Ranald Slidell Mackenzie, Indian Fighting Cavalryman." *Southwestern Historical Quarterly*, LVI (January, 1953), 378–396.

Williams, J. W. "The Butterfield Overland Mail Road Across Texas." *Southwestern Historical Quarterly*, LXI (July, 1957), 1–19.

BOOKS

Allred, B. W.; Dykes, J. C.; Goodwyn, Frank; and Simms, D. Harper, eds. *Great Western Indian Fights*. Lincoln: University of Nebraska Press, 1960.

Andrist, Ralph K. *The Long Death: The Last Days of the Plains Indian*. New York: The Macmillan Company, 1964.

Athearn, Robert G. *William Tecumseh Sherman and the Settlement of the West*. Norman: University of Oklahoma Press, 1956.

Barrett, John G. *Sherman's March Through the Carolinas*. Chapel Hill: The University of North Carolina Press, 1956.

Bentley, George R. *A History of the Freedmen's Bureau*. Philadelphia: University of Pennsylvania Press, 1955.

Biddle, Ellen McGowan. *Reminiscences of a Soldier's Wife*. Philadelphia: J. B. Lippincott Company, 1907.

Billington, Ray Allen. *Westward Expansion: A History of the American Frontier*. New York: The Macmillan Company, 1960.

Bourke, John G. *On the Border with Crook*. New York: Charles Scribner's Sons, 1891.

Brimlow, George F. *Cavalryman Out of the West*. Caldwell, Idaho: The Caxton Printers, Ltd., 1944.

Buck, Paul H. *The Road to Reunion*. Boston: Little, Brown and Company, 1937.

Butler, Benjamin F. *Private and Official Correspondence of General Benjamin F. Butler: During the Period of the Civil War*. 5 vols. Norwood, Massachusetts: The Plimpton Press, 1917.

Byrne, P. E. *Soldiers of the Plains*. New York: Minton, Balch and Company, 1926.

Carrington, Frances C. *My Army Life and the Fort Phil. Kearney Massacre*. Philadelphia: J. B. Lippincott Company, 1910.

Carter, Hodding. *The Angry Scar: The Story of Reconstruction*. New York: Doubleday and Company, 1959.

Commager, Henry Steele. *The American Mind: An Interpretation of American Thought and Character Since the 1880's*. New Haven: Yale University Press, 1950.

Cornish, Dudley T. *The Sable Arm: Negro Troops in the Union Army, 1861–1865*. New York: W. W. Norton and Company, 1966.

Crook, George. *General George Crook: His Autobiography*. Edited by Martin F. Schmitt. Norman: University of Oklahoma Press, 1960.

Custer, Elizabeth B. *Boots and Saddles*. New York: Harper and Brothers Publishers, 1889.

———. *Tenting on the Plains*. New York: Charles Webster and Company, 1887.

Custer, George Armstrong. *My Life on the Plains, or Personal Experiences with Indians*. New York: Sheldon and Company, 1874.

De-Forest, John William. *A Union Officer in the Reconstruction*. Edited by James H. Croushore and David M. Potter. New Haven: Yale University Press, 1948.

Department of the Army. *American Military History, 1607–1958*. Washington: Government Printing Office, 1959.

Downey, Fairfax. *Indian-Fighting Army*. New York: Bantam Books, 1963.

Eaton, John. *Grant, Lincoln and the Freedmen: Reminiscences of the Civil War*. New York: Longmans, Green, and Company, 1907.

Ewers, John C. *The Blackfeet: Raiders of the Northwestern Plains*. Norman: University of Oklahoma Press, 1958.

Fey, Harold W., and McNickle, D'Arcy. *Indians and Other Americans*. New York: Harper and Brothers, 1959.

Foreman, Grant. *A History of Oklahoma*. Norman: University of Oklahoma Press, 1945.

Forsyth, George A. *The Story of the Soldier.* New York: D. Appleton and Company, 1900.

Franklin, John Hope. *From Slavery to Freedom: A History of Negro Americans.* New York: Alfred A. Knopf, 1967.

Frazer, Robert W. *Forts of the West.* Norman: University of Oklahoma Press, 1965.

Frink, Maurice, and Barthelmess, Casey E. *Photographer on An Army Mule.* Norman: University of Oklahoma Press, 1965.

Fritz, Henry E. *The Movement for Indian Assimilation.* Philadelphia: University of Pennsylvania Press, 1963.

Ganoe, William Addleman. *The History of the United States Army.* New York: D. Appleton and Company, 1924.

Hagan, William T. *American Indians.* Chicago: The University of Chicago Press, 1961.

Hart, B. H. Liddell. *Sherman: Soldier, Realist, American.* New York: Dodd, Mead and Company, 1929.

Higginson, Thomas Wentworth. *Army Life in a Black Regiment.* New York: Collier Books, 1962.

Historical and Pictorial Review, 24th Infantry Regiment. Baton Rouge: Army and Navy Publishing Company, 1941.

Howe, M. A. DeWolfe, ed. *Home Letters of General Sherman.* New York: Charles Scribner's Sons, 1909.

Hyde, George E. *A Sioux Chronicle.* Norman: University of Oklahoma Press, 1956.

Johnson, Virginia Weisel. *The Unregimented General: A Biography of Nelson A. Miles.* Boston: Houghton Mifflin Company, 1962.

Johnson, W. Fletcher. *Life of Sitting Bull and History of the Indian War of 1890–91.* Philadelphia: Edgewood Publishing Company, 1891.

Katz, William L. *Teachers' Guide to American Negro History.* Chicago: Quadrangle Books, 1968.

Keim, De B. Randolph. *Sheridan's Troopers on the Borders: A Winter Campaign on the Plains.* New York: George Routledge and Sons, 1885.

Kelly, Alfred H., and Harbinson, Winfred. *The American Constitution: Its Origin and Development.* New York: W. W. Norton and Company, 1963.

Knight, Oliver. *Following the Indian Wars.* Norman: University of Oklahoma Press, 1960.

Lamar, Howard Roberts. *Dakota Territory, 1861–1889: A Study of Frontier Politics.* New Haven: Yale University Press, 1956.

Leckie, William H. *The Buffalo Soldiers: A Narrative of the Negro Cavalry in the West.* Norman: University of Oklahoma Press, 1967

Lee, Irvin H. *Negro Medal of Honor Men.* New York: Dodd, Mead and Company, 1967.

Lewis, Lloyd. *Sherman: Fighting Prophet.* New York: Harcourt, Brace and Company, 1932.

Logan, Rayford W. *The Betrayal of the Negro from Rutherford B. Hayes to Woodrow Wilson.* New York: Collier Books, 1965.

Lummis, Charles R. *General Crook and the Apache Wars.* Flagstaff, Arizona: Northland Press, 1966.

McCracken, Harold, ed. *Frederic Remington's Own West.* New York: The Dial Press, 1960.

McKitrick, Eric L. *Andrew Johnson and Reconstruction.* Chicago: The University of Chicago Press, 1960.

McPherson, James M. *The Negro's Civil War: How American Negroes Felt and Acted During the War for the Union.* New York: Vintage Books, 1967.

McReynolds, Edwin C. *Oklahoma: A History of the Sooner State.* Norman: University of Oklahoma Press, 1954.

Miles, Nelson A. *Personal Recollections of General Nelson A. Miles.* New York: The Werner Company, 1896.

———. *Serving the Republic.* New York: Harper and Brothers, 1911.

Morgan, H. Wayne, ed. *The Gilded Age: A Reappraisal.* Syracuse University Press, 1963.

Nankivell, John H. *History of the Twenty-fifth Regiment, United States Infantry, 1869–1926.* Denver: Smith-Brooks Printing Company, 1926.

Ormsby, Waterman L. *The Butterfield Overland Mail.* Edited by Lyle H. Wright and Josephine M. Bynum. San Marino, California: The Huntington Library, 1960.

Powell, William H. *List of Officers of the Army of the United*

States from 1779 to 1900. New York: L. R. Hamersly and Company, 1900.

Pratt, Richard Henry. *Battlefield and Classroom: Four Decades with the American Indians, 1867–1904.* New Haven: Yale University Press, 1964.

Quarles, Benjamin. *The Negro in the Civil War.* Boston: Little, Brown and Company, 1953.

———. *The Negro in the Making of America.* New York: Collier Books, 1968.

Radin, Paul. *The Story of the American Indian.* New York: Liveright Publishing Corporation, 1927.

Randall, J. G. and Donald, David. *The Civil War and Reconstruction.* Boston: D. C. Heath and Company, 1961.

Rickey, Don, Jr. *Forty Miles a Day on Beans and Hay: The Enlisted Soldier Fighting the Indian Wars.* Norman: University of Oklahoma Press, 1963.

Rister, Carl Coke. *Fort Griffin on the Texas Frontier.* Norman: University of Oklahoma Press, 1956.

———. *Land Hunger: David L. Payne and the Oklahoma Boomers.* Norman: University of Oklahoma Press, 1942.

———. *The Southwestern Frontier, 1865–1881.* Cleveland: The Arthur H. Clark Company, 1928.

Roe, Frank Gilbert. *The Indian and The Horse.* Norman: University of Oklahoma Press, 1955.

Sanders, Helen Fitzgerald. *A History of Montana.* 3 vols. Chicago: The Lewis Publishing Company, 1913.

Sefton, James E. *The United States Army and Reconstruction, 1865–1877.* Baton Rouge: Louisiana State University Press, 1967.

Sheridan, Philip H. *Personal Memoirs of P. H. Sheridan.* 2 vols. New York: Charles L. Webster and Company, 1888.

Sherman, John. *John Sherman's Recollections of Forty Years in The House, Senate and Cabinet.* 2 vols. New York: The Werner Company, 1895.

Sherman, William T. *Memoirs of General W. T. Sherman.* 2 vols. New York: Webster and Company, 1891.

Singletary, Otis A. *Negro Militia and Reconstruction.* Austin: University of Texas Press, 1957.

Stampp, Kenneth M. *The Peculiar Institution: Slavery in the Ante-Bellum South.* New York: Vintage Books, 1956.

Summerhayes, Martha. *Vanished Arizona: Recollections of My Army Life.* Salem, Massachusetts: The Salem Press Company, 1911.

Tebbel, John. *A Compact History of the Indian Wars.* New York: Hawthorn Books, Inc., 1966.

Thomas, Benjamin P. and Hyman, Harold M. *Stanton: The Life and Times of Lincoln's Secretary of War.* New York: Alfred A. Knopf, 1962.

Thorndike, Rachel Sherman, ed. *The Sherman Letters: Correspondence Between General and Senator Sherman from 1837 to 1891.* London: Sampson Low, Marston, and Company, 1894.

Utley, Robert M. *The Last Days of the Sioux Nation.* New Haven: Yale University Press, 1963.

Vestal, Stanley. *New Sources of Indian History, 1850–1891.* Norman: University of Oklahoma Press, 1934.

————. *Sitting Bull: Champion of the Sioux.* Norman: University of Oklahoma Press, 1957.

Webb, Walter Prescott. *The Great Plains.* New York: Grosset and Dunlap, 1931.

Weigley, Russell F. *History of The United States Army.* New York: The Macmillan Company, 1967.

Wellman, Paul, I. *Death on the Prairie.* New York: Pyramid Books, 1947.

————. *Death on the Desert.* New York: Pyramid Books, 1947.

West Point Alumni Foundation. *Register of Graduates and Former Cadets of the United States Military Academy.* West Point: The West Point Alumni Foundation, Inc., 1964.

Whisenhunt, Donald W. *Fort Richardson: Outpost on the Texas Frontier.* Southwestern Studies, Vol. V, No. 4, Monograph No. 20. El Paso: Texas Western Press, 1968.

Wiley, Bell Irvin. *The Life of Billy Yank: The Common Soldier of the Union.* New York: The Bobbs-Merrill Company, 1952.

Woodward, C. Vann. *The Strange Career of Jim Crow.* New York: Oxford University Press, 1957.

Wyman, Walker D. *The Wild Horse of the West*. Lincoln: University of Nebraska Press, 1945.

NEWSPAPERS

Great Falls Tribune. 1888–1891.
Missoula Gazette. 1888–1891.
New York Times. 1863, 1866–1878.
Rising Sun. 1888–1891.
Stock Growers Journal. 1890–1891.
Weekly Missoulian. 1888–1891.

OTHER MATERIALS

Hoge, William M., Jr. "The Logistical System of the U.S. Army During the Indian Wars, 1866–1899." Master's thesis, Washington State University, 1968.

Index

Desertion, 60, 78–79, 86–87, 127, 137–138, 145
Disciples of Christ Church, 94
Discrimination, 16, 26, 146. *See also* prejudice
District of the Pecos, 38
Dodge City, Kansas, 75–76
Douglass, Frederick, 11
Downey, Fairfax, 6

Eagle Springs, Texas, 37
Edmunds, Senator George, 125
El Muerto Station, Texas, 26
El Paso Mail Lines, 26
El Paso, Mexico, 22
El Paso, Texas, 128
Endicott, Secretary of War W. C., 80

Fifth Cavalry, 79
Fifty-ninth U.S. Colored Infantry Regiment, 93
First Cavalry, 131
First Infantry, 138
Flathead Indian Reservation, 64
Flathead Lake, Montana Territory, 65
Forsyth, Maj. George A., 7
Fort Apache, Arizona Territory, 81
Fort Bayard, New Mexico Territory, 81–83, 85, 105
Fort Bliss, Texas, 19, 43n, 96
Fort Clark, Texas, 19–22, 94, 98
description of, 20–21
Fort Concho, Texas, 22, 29, 32, 43n, 50, 128

Fort Custer, Montana Territory, 60, 66, 131
Fort Davis, Texas, 19, 21–22, 24, 27, 29, 50, 94–97, 99, 128
Fort Dodge, Kansas, 75
Fort Duncan, Texas, 19, 23, 32, 121
Fort Elliott, Texas, 74–76, 79–80
Fort Grant, Arizona Territory, 81, 83–85
Fort Griffin, Texas, 29
Fort Hale, Dakota Territory, 50–51, 131
Fort Keogh, Montana, 69, 134
Fort Leavenworth, Kansas, 79, 130
Fort McIntosh, Texas, 29
Fort McKavitt, Texas, 17, 19, 126
Fort Meade, Dakota Territory, 50–52, 58–59
Fort Missoula, Montana Territory, 60, 64–65, 67–68
Fort Phil Kearney, Wyoming, 66
Fort Quitman, Texas, 19, 22, 30, 37, 43n, 128
Fort Randall, Dakota Territory, 50, 52–53, 56, 129
Fort Reno, Indian Territory, 74, 76
Fort Richardson, Texas, 29
Fort Shaw, Montana Territory, 60–62, 134
Fort Sill, Indian Territory, 23, 30, 74, 80
Fort Sisseton, Dakota Territory, 61